Gliding

From passenger to pilot

Steven Longland

Second edition

The Crowood Press

First published in 2001 by
The Crowood Press Ltd
Ramsbury, Marlborough
Wiltshire SN8 2HR

Revised edition 2012

www.crowood.com

British Library Cataloguing-in-Publication Data
A catalogue record for this book is available from the British Library.

ISBN 978 1 84797 393 1

Acknowledgements
A number of the illustrations in this book have appeared previously in *Sailplane* and *Gliding* (UK gliding's official magazine), and/or in training material provided by the BGA. They were drawn by the author of this book, who is grateful to both of the above for allowing him to 'replay' them here and so save himself a lot of time.

My thanks again to the beta-readers, Penny in particular, for ploughing through the chaff of earlier drafts in search of wheat, and to all of them for those interesting suggestions which were possible! Many thanks also to the very generous people who have allowed me to use their excellent photographs without charge.

Special thanks to my brother Simon, who created a 3D model of an ASK21, which has been used as the basis for many of the illustrations.

Designed and typeset by Guy Croton

Printed and bound in Malaysia by Times Offset (M) Sdn Bhd

Contents

Introduction

Of all the dreams of mankind, flight has to have been one of the very best. Like much else, success and familiarity have reduced it to another rather humdrum piece of technical furniture. Yet, as any half-decent pilot will tell you – if they can keep a grip on their embarrassment – the dream-like qualities that made the idea of flight so compelling in the first place still exist. They are part of mankind's symbolic pursuit of freedom and remain as powerful as ever; promising the possibility of escape, however temporary, and a teasing glimpse of what it must be like not to be forever stuck by the feet to our own dark shadow.

Gliding, as part of sporting aviation, offers a vast range of experiences, from the unusual and stunningly beautiful to the occasionally rather average and intensely frustrating – as illustrated by the following description of two contrasting flights.

ANGELS TWO ONE

The radio is off: there is no need to speak to anyone at the moment. The distracting chatter rippling out of other gliders flying across country hundreds of miles further south seemed to be largely about lunch and sand-wiches, and questions about whether John has set off to retrieve Mike from yet another off-field landing. The slightly irritating squeak of the variometer's audio – the reedy little 'voice' of the instrument that tells the pilot whether the glider is climbing or not – has also been silenced: the needle on the dial says 'going up', which is enough. As tellingly, the air through which the glider is flying has been well ironed somewhere during its travels: even the minute tremblings of turbulence that can be felt and heard in the smoothest air lower down have completely vanished.

The glider responds to all of this by being whisper quiet, seemingly suspended in the bright and secret centre of the world. A few barely audible background sounds remain, reminding you that this is the real world: the subdued rush of the airflow over the glider, the gentle hiss of the oxygen entering the rubbery-smelling face mask via a small balloon that swells and collapses rhythmically with each breath, and every so often a creak from the perspex canopy as it contracts in the cold.

Slowly the altimeter winds through 18,000ft. Is this the day finally to gain the third and last Diamond for the coveted Diamond badge? Not quite there yet: it needs a gain of height above the release from the launch of at least 16,400ft. Past attempts have included several 'not quite there' moments – rising into the gloomy centre of large clouds where strong lift can propel the glider upwards at huge speeds, to emerge suddenly with a bright visual 'pop' from the side of a snow-white tower into brilliant sunshine at 15,000ft, or 10,000ft – always just short of that magic figure.

It is an hour since take-off from the Deeside club's site at Aboyne in Scotland. After release from the aerotow the flight was a bumpy ride in the rising air below the cumulus clouds, quickly spiralling up to their base at 3,500ft – then a dash forwards through the swirling fringes of one cloud's upwind edge to make contact with the lee wave off Morven. Millions of tons of air blow against the western edge of this hill and are forced upwards; once over the summit this enormous mass of air then plunges downwards – but if the weather conditions are right, as they are today, it bounces up and then falls again. Like the ripples trailing downstream of a large and barely submerged stone in a swiftly flowing river, these gigantic standing waves form a train which can stretch for hundreds of miles. In other parts of the world where the mountains are higher, these waves can rise to well over 50,000ft. On this day every hill in Scotland is trig-gering a wave, resulting in a complicated pattern of aerial hills and valleys which, marked by cloud or not, are like elegantly smoothed, often exaggerated, but occasionally rather approximate copies of the ups and downs of the ground below.

In wave.

Unlike past attempts at Diamond height there is no need to 'fly on the instruments', head down in the whirring cockpit, submerged in a cold and damp world of grey. Today the sun beats down – but although the cockpit seems warm, cold feet remain a problem because they are hidden in the darkness under the instrument panel. Thicker socks would have been a good idea.

From the ground, the 50ft span glider, facing into a 45kt westerly wind, is hard to see, little more than a tiny motionless white cross set into the brilliant blue ceramic of the sky – but from the cramped cockpit the pilot is presented with a view that is spectacularly vast. This is not peeping sideways out of the tiny, prison-like window of a commercial airliner, but being immersed in an immense and archetypal landscape through which it is possible to move almost as you wish. Far away to the south lies Edinburgh, hidden in the gloomy depths beneath an unbroken sheet of dense and blindingly white cloud. To the north the air is incredibly clear and dotted randomly, way below, with flocks of small, sheep-like cumulus clouds. Just visible in the far distance are Elgin, Inverness, and the curve of the east coast which leads from the Moray Firth, away to John O'Groats.

The dividing line between the starched linen-white world to the south and the richly stippled realm of greens and browns to the north lies straight down the Dee valley. Flying directly above this division creates an odd sensation, as if the glider and pilot are stitching the two halves together. Yet what overwhelms this odd yet not entirely untruthful conceit of the brain is not so much the view – which is of glass-like clarity – but the extraordinary stillness.

The altimeter needle crawls past 21,000ft – enough height to gain that final Diamond, and with sufficient margin to make it certain. The silence is unbroken by applause.

THE HAIRSHIRT IMPERATIVE

By contrast it is the middle of summer, at Gransden Lodge near Cambridge. The sky is blue and slightly hazy, the visibility rather poor, and the wind fresh from the east. By about midday the sun has done its best to create the upgoing currents of air or thermals that gliders need to stay airborne over the region's chessboard landscape. When the thermals do finally appear they are rough, as if quality control has taken the day off – probably gone to the seaside to escape the heat. Someone already airborne has reported that none of the thermals has so far reached beyond about 2,500ft, and even from the ground pilots can see that today cross country flying, even soaring locally, is going to be hard work. But there we are - if you like cross country flying you will go and do it even if the conditions are difficult, and occasionally just because they are.

First a winch launch. There are none of the helpful cumulus clouds which usually signpost rising air, so it is a bee-line away from the airfield towards a faint and milky patch of haze in the sky which indicates a possible thermal. The glider feels skittish and the air is full of subdued noises and bumps and thumps a-plenty, as if herds of small grumpy animals were charging past, insulting each other as they go. This is rather bad news, because a usable thermal requires billions of these turbulent little beasts – the air molecules – to act together on a grand scale. It seems an impossible coincidence that they should ever do this, but luckily it is nothing of the sort; though whether they will co-operate in time to prevent a return to the airfield and an early landing is another matter.

Abruptly the glider bounces upwards. As if it has been suddenly pinched, the audio lets out a startled squeak, indicating that the glider is climbing and must now be banked swiftly and steeply to spiral tightly into the very narrow central area of good 'lift', a normal feature of thermals. Today these are narrower than usual, and the direction in which the blustery wind is blowing at different heights has cut into each one and shredded the rising air into jolting and disjointed fragments so that one moment the glider is climbing, the next it is not. The audio registers 'up' in a series of desperately unmusical and stuttering blips – like morse code stuck on the dots – and then shortly afterwards 'down', which comes out as a suitably mournful wail of despair. Judging by the occasional gleeful and smug little burble it makes, it seems to be taking some joy in all the teasing.

Gliding is a wonderful sport, but on days like these you can sometimes find yourself wondering why you bothered to take off at all. After about three hours of being bumped around, never climbing fast nor managing to rise above 2,800ft (and only getting that high once, just), nor having travelled very far away – 'Well I never, there's the airfield again!' – and unable to shelter from the sun's unrelenting blaze in the cool grey shadow of a cloud, is it time to give in and land? The water bottle is empty, and in terms of vigour and enthusiasm, so is the pilot.

Gliders circling in a blue thermal.

60 miles visibility. A fairly rare occurrence in the UK.

Your non-gliding friends will tell you what a fantastic day they had at the seaside – amazingly all the children behaved themselves – and say cheerfully, 'Must have been good gliding!' Indeed it was, you might reply with the merest hint of sarcasm, but somewhere else in the world. Still, such a trial of a flight has provided opportunities for self-improvement and keeping in practice, has advanced one's understanding of the atmosphere and how it behaves, and increased one's appreciation of the glider's delightful handling qualities – and no doubt done many other equally elevating things. But enough is enough, and now, with a clear conscience of duty done, landing can be made.

Such 'improving' days are relatively rare, but while one might complain about them, nothing can be done – this is the weather, after all – and from a pilot's point of view there is always something to be gained from flying in less than optimum conditions. Exactly what, though, can sometimes be debatable.

1 The Early Days

Although balloons had taken to the air by 1786, and blown away in the wind much as they have done ever since, it took nearly seventy years before steerable and navigable balloons, known as dirigibles, became a reality. And it was more than fifty years after that before true powered, heavier-than-air flight was achieved.

The road to heavier-than-air flight was not to be an easy one. First, there was the complete lack of a relatively light and powerful engine. That did not arrive until Nickolaus Otto invented the internal (petrol) combustion engine in 1876. Second, almost all of the extensive body of aerodynamic and structural knowledge that is fundamental to successful heavier-than-air flight simply didn't exist. Thirdly, very few people had the time, money or the inclination to devote themselves to solving any of these problems.

Sporadic attempts at flight had taken place throughout recorded history. The myth of Daedalus and Icarus may have some basis in fact, but it is more of a finger-wagging moral tale than a technical description of structural meltdown. Most of the attempts at flight before 1800, and about which we know, were characterized by the often fatal triumph of faith over intelligence. One cannot deny the foolhardy courage of some of the earliest attempts, but essential to success is imagination and practicality, plus a generous splash of unemotional common sense. One of the first people to be interested in heavier-than-air flight and to have all these qualities in anything like safe proportions,

plus the analytical brain to go with them, was the Yorkshire baronet Sir George Cayley.

Sir George, who was born in 1773 and died of old age in 1857, was the first person to outline exactly what was required for flight, and to have some practical and positive results in that area. Most of his predecessors had attempted, with a complete lack of success, to imitate the birds. Jump from a high place, flap furiously and hope for the best was about as far as most of them went – and in a downward direction.

Cayley knew that these types of antics relied far too much on luck, and that a more cautious and thought-out approach would have more success. He also knew that we weren't strong enough to fly by flapping. However, he did not, as he could have done (and no doubt been applauded for his good sense), give up on heavier-than-air flight. He realized that regardless of what the birds were doing, we did not have to flap to fly; all we had to do was utilize the same basic principles as the bird itself was using. In other words, we could have a fixed wing for 'lift', add an engine to create the necessary forward movement, and treat the two as separate items.

Air may surround and keep us alive but it is (a) invisible and (b), by comparison with water, apparently incapable of supporting anything heavier than a cloud or a balloon. Without belittling the major advance that balloons represented, lighter-than-air flight was relatively straightforward. People knew that objects could be made to float in

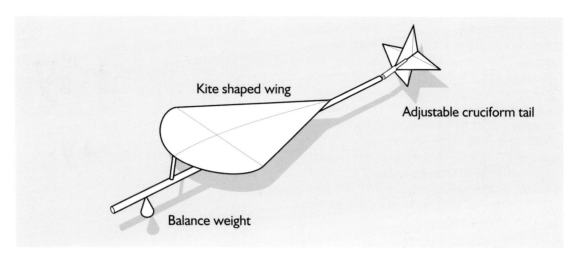

Cayley's 1804 model glider.

water, and there was no reason to suppose that a machine couldn't be made that floated in the air, thin though it was. Heavier-than-air flight was something else altogether. Air's invisibility was bad enough, but worse, much of the traditional theory behind how things worked was based upon the words of long dead Greek philosophers, and was just plain wrong. There's no guarantee that what we know today is correct but most theories appear to fit the reality better now, and if they don't they are replaced.

Cayley built several gliders, beginning in 1804 with a model which bears a striking resemblance to contemporary chuck-gliders, and a small biplane glider that is alleged to have carried a ten-year-old boy. His aeronautical researches and writings continued in fits and starts throughout his long and immensely busy life, and in 1852, when he was seventy, he built a man-carrying glider in which he persuaded his coachman, John Appleby, to fly. The glider was launched from one side of a small valley in Yorkshire by several strong men, flew swiftly and smoothly to the other side and crashed. Appleby, unhurt, told Sir George that he had been hired to drive, not fly, and resigned on the spot. In terms of further advances in practical aviation that was just about it for many years.

When suitable engines were not available the only research vehicles, whether models or not, had to be gliders. The original aim was always powered flight, and gliding just one step along the way to what was regarded as the more serious goal. Gliding was just a bit – well, rather childish!

This view of gliding as toy aviation is unfortunately still fairly common, even among people who ought to know better, and as witless now as it was then. Had suitable engines been around, things would undoubtedly have been different, but for many of the pioneers that fact probably saved their lives.

The press and public attitude to heavier-than-air flight, when it existed at all, was almost entirely negative. What attracted attention, then as now, was the toying with danger – just as long as the watchers themselves weren't likely to be involved in the results. Huge crowds attended both balloon launchings and public executions – the distinction between the two being sometimes a bit vague. But if fireworks and death captured public attention, what had aeroplanes to offer? Absolutely nothing because, in the general view, nobody had ever made one that worked. Might as well try and fly the washerwoman's wicker laundry basket! Yet, even though a powered aircraft hadn't flown, and wouldn't do so until 1903, Cayley's gliders had already done so, though the flights were all short.

He was well aware of what would today be classed as an image problem. Replying to a correspondent in 1809, he wrote in mild exasperation (he was too even-handed a man to become incandescent), of 'the art of flying, or aerial navigation, as I have chosen to term it for the sake of giving a little more dignity to a subject bordering upon the ludicrous in public estimation'.

All of the most successful early experimenters, including Otto Lilienthal (1848–96), understood the value of models and testing. Lilienthal had none of today's sophisticated equipment but, like Cayley before him, he knew that flight was an area where guesswork could easily prove fatal. Lilienthal made many flights in his various gliders, which he controlled by shifting his weight, like a modern hang glider pilot. Of all his many contributions to heavier-than–air flight, one of the more important, if inadvertent, was to be the first person to be photographed 'aviating' successfully. The resultant publicity had an almost wholly positive effect, and proved to a previously thoroughly unimpressed public that aeroplanes might very well work, exactly as the madmen had been saying all along.

Nevertheless, despite changes in public attitudes, and the new enthusiasm generated among other researchers, success remained frustratingly elusive. *The Boys Book of Aeroplanes* of 1912 summed up the six-year period between Lilienthal's unfortunate death in a crash and the Wright brothers' eventual success, as follows:

At this stage in the history of aviation the student finds himself in the midst of considerable confusion. Ideas old, worn out, fantastic or ludicrous are mingled with a mass of good experimental and theoretical work that is stultified by want of money and by want of motive power. Thus, because there was no means of ascertaining the real value of any theory, the work was done over and over again and continued in periodical resurrection until early in the twentieth century...

A few names stand out in that period. Among them was the Frenchman Alphonse Penaud (1850–80) whose suicide at the age of thirty, from a mixture of ill-health and despair, removed from the scene one of the most brilliant and original experimenters of the time. The Englishman, Percy Pilcher, was continuing Lilienthal's experiments and on the verge of adding a carbonic acid motor to what was, in fact, a hang glider, when he was killed in a flying accident.

Then came the Wright brothers, Orville and Wilbur. Oddly, most of the aerial experimenters before them – with the exception of Cayley and the others already mentioned – were utterly obsessed with making an aeroplane that was so well behaved in the air that it didn't, in effect, need a pilot at all. To these people the notion of any form of control was entirely foreign. Had any of their machines become airborne, the pilot's influence on the subsequent course of

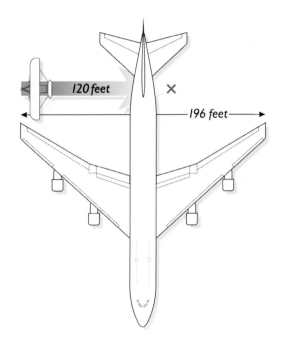

Distance of Wright brothers' first powered flight.

the flight would have been zero. There are occasions when, with hindsight, it is clear that everything would have turned out a great deal better if the pilot hadn't been allowed any say at all. But we would all agree that if we buy a new car, for example, it is very nice if it comes with a steering wheel that works.

The Wrights decided from the outset that they needed a controllable aeroplane, and then made things very difficult for themselves by choosing one of the most unstable configurations possible, tail-first. That aside, a large part of their success was due to their meticulous research and testing. They knew also that piloting skills were vital. Weight shift did not seem to them to be an ideal method of control and over several years they researched and developed a system broadly similar to that used by today's aircraft, but it was definitely the hard knocks 'crash-bang-try-it-again' school of 'how to be a pilot'. Luckily these days, learning to fly isn't quite so DIY, but had the Wrights not learnt skilful control of their gliders, their very first powered flight would almost certainly have been a disaster.

On a windy day in December 1903, Orville made the first controlled powered heavier-than-air flight in the world. It lasted all of 12 secs and covered about 120ft – rather less than the wingspan of a Boeing 747. Had there been no wind the flight would have been about 550ft (shorter than Lilienthal's longest glides). Subsequent flights on the same day were longer, with the final one lasting 59 secs and covering a distance over the ground of about half a mile. Their 'Flyer' sustained minor damage during the last landing, and shortly after it was returned to their base camp on the dunes for repairs, it was blown over by a gust of wind and seriously damaged.

Sporting Gliding

Parting of the ways?

Despite its idealism, the dream of flight was, like most human dreams, never entirely innocent. To fly freely like the birds, without a care in the world etc, was the main intent, yet it always had about it a strong whiff of the commercial. The idea of travelling quickly to any part of the globe, there to trade and then return, preferably with profit, was a powerful one that has not changed over the years. Neither has 'quickly' changed much. It remains the relative word it has always been. Even in the year 2012 it takes nearly 24 hours of commercially sponsored discomfort, trapped in the aerial equivalent of a mediaeval torture chamber and mobile petri dish, to reach Australia or New Zealand. Aircraft can now go just about anywhere in almost any kind of weather, and are even starting to look after themselves.

Bit by bit, engineers are turning professional pilots into aerial couch potatoes. By comparison, sporting aviation, gliding in particular, is hands-on flying and the pilot is responsible for just about everything that happens.

The appeal of motorless flight is quite difficult to describe. It is partly a game of energy management that requires skill for success, but there is also a sufficient element of luck and the unexpected to keep your attention and jazz up what could otherwise become either routine or, if your skill was never quite sufficient, rather depressing.

There is also the feeling, as there must have been in all aviation in the early days, of contact with the living and invisible body of the air, and there is a very tactile relationship between it and the pilot and glider. There are the panoramic views, the light of the sun on the clouds, the wonderfully varied quilt of field and shadow, and the endlessly subtle variations in colour. The world appears very tidy and trouble free from up above, wrapped all about by the thin, almost threadbare protective coat of an atmosphere randomly patterned by the weather: constantly changing, independent, full of surprises, and the unreliable provider of the fuel that gliders need to stay airborne.

There were, and probably always will be, people who like the idea of making use of some of the essentially free energy available in the air, and who appreciate also the blend of intellectual and physical skills required to make the best out of what is available. Yet a common factor relating to all the motorless airsports, and probably very much in the minds of the earliest exponents of sporting

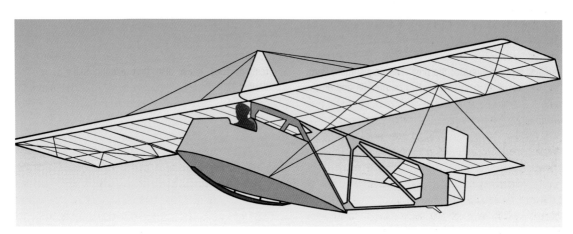

Zogling primary glider.

gliding, remains cost. Powered flight can be very expensive. Gliding clubs were set up by enthusiasts to reduce their individual costs, and they operated like friendly societies owning several gliders which individual members, in effect, rented out.

The first gliding clubs in the UK were set up after the First World War, following several gliding 'meets' that attracted large numbers of spectators. By 1930 there were about fifty gliding clubs dotted around the UK, and known to be operational by the British Gliding Association, itself founded in 1929 to promote the sport of gliding.

EVOLUTION

It was inevitable that demands for better performance, largely based on the desire for longer flights, would fuel technical advance, and between the twentieth century's two World Wars the sporting glider gradually evolved from a basic flying machine into something elegant, light, and extremely efficient. New forms of lifting air were discovered and flight distances went from a few miles, to fifty, then a hundred, then to three hundred. The challenge to do just a bit better each time and discover something new, was one which always was and hopefully always will be irresistible. Ironically, one of the bigger boosts to the gliding movement came as a result of the First World War. At the cessation of hostilities in 1918, the Treaty of Versailles forbade the Germans an air force, but in the 1930s the fledgling and secret Luftwaffe sidestepped this restriction by using the gliding clubs to train its pilots.

By the late 1930s there was talk of gliding becoming an Olympic sport. Indeed, the decision was taken to introduce it during the event scheduled for 1940. To give every competitor a level playing field, ie to measure pilot ability rather than glider performance, the Meise, designed and built in Germany, was chosen to be the first of what it was assumed would be an Olympic breed. Darker and less happy things were in the wind, unfortunately, and the Second World War put a stop to all that. Gliding still isn't an Olympic event, probably because it is neither a spectator sport, nor particularly 'instant' like football or athletics. Even so, modern developments in electronics (on-board cameras and the like) could change all that, and there have already been Internet based 'from the front' reports of gliding competitions.

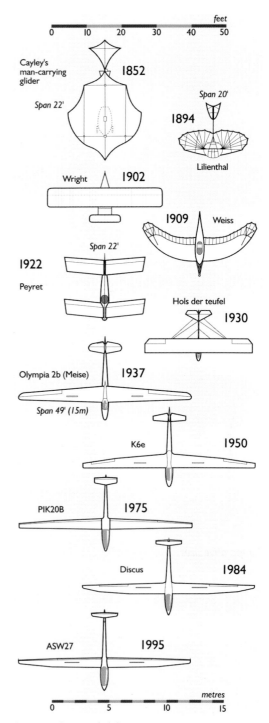

Changing shapes of gliders.

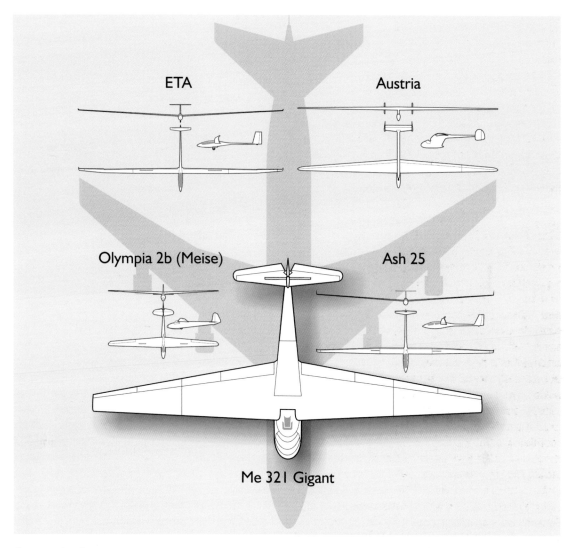

ETA

Austria

Olympia 2b (Meise)

Ash 25

Me 321 Gigant

Comparative sizes.

MILITARY USES OF GLIDERS

Gliding in wartime

During the war, sporting gliding was obviously put on hold, but gliders were built in vast numbers to carry troops and ordnance. The Germans had originally pioneered their military use, and during D-Day the Allies used gliders in vast numbers. Some of the film footage from the period, with landing areas littered with scores of shattered gliders, would make any modern club's Chief Flying Instructor (not to mention the Treasurer) weep. As for the troops who had to go into battle in these disposable machines, they probably looked upon their flights as toboggan rides to hell.

For the intended invasion of Britain in 1940, the Germans had built one of the largest gliders ever seen, the Me323 Gigant. This monster had a span of 180ft (55m) – 16ft less than a standard 747 – and a maximum take-off weight of 94,799lb (43,000kg). Towing it was a risky business.

An ASH-25 two-seat glider over the Barres des Ecrins in the southern French alps. J. BRIDGE

Eventually the scale and danger of the whole exercise proved too much, and the Gigant was fitted with six engines of its own and left to look after itself. Although completely irrelevant to sporting gliding, the Gigant does nevertheless represent one of the extremes to which gliders have been taken.

Gargantuanism has afflicted sporting gliding at various other times, and in 1930 one of the largest soaring gliders ever built was a one-off called the Austria, which had a span of 98ft (30m). Modern gliders like the ASH25 or the Nimbus 4 have a span of 25m. The latest and largest sporting glider ever, the ETA, first flew at Magdeburg in Germany, on 3 July 2000; its span is 99ft 8in (30.4m).

At the other end of the scale are very small gliders like the Hutter 17, with a span of 32ft (9.69m), the first example of which was built in 1934. The photograph on the next page will give you a clearer idea of its scale – the person in the picture is 5ft 4in.

Post World War Two Gliding in the UK

By the end of the Second World War Europe had been devastated and the UK was technically bankrupt. Hard and depressing times lay ahead, and in the UK rationing and shortages of one sort or another remained facts of life until the early 1950s. Nevertheless, pre-war sporting gliders both in Britain and abroad, which had mysteriously vanished at the outset of hostilities, began to reappear. As the UK's economy improved, and things began to look brighter, interest in air sports in general revived. Pre-war clubs dragged themselves to their feet again and new ones appeared, helped by the energy and enthusiasm of pre-war glider pilots.

Surprisingly, gliding had its most remarkable renaissance in Germany, a country that lay in ruins and was broken in two. Out of the wreckage there gradually emerged a strong gliding movement and what were to become some of the best known designers and glider manufacturers in the world. In the tradition of Lilienthal, there were and are aeronautical research facilities attached to some German universities which design and build one-off sailplanes (such as the ETA mentioned earlier) as student projects and/or as part of general aerodynamic research. The UK did have a flourishing glider industry of its own until 1972, when the last surviving UK builder of gliders, Slingsby Sailplanes, dropped out of the picture. Today, Germany is the only country in the world which designs, produces and exports gliders in any appreciable volume.

As for the future, there are still records to break and advances to be made. Technical excellence has increased glider performance beyond anything anyone

A Hutter 17, first built in 1934.

ever thought possible, but it has come at a high price. There are signs that the co-operative element, which was such a strong feature of the early clubs, is being eroded by increasing private ownership – which in itself is partly a response to the increased pressures on people's time. In both respects the smaller clubs tend to be less affected. As a result gliding faces new challenges, but the original impetus of the sport, its soul if you like, remains untouched. The challenge and beauty are as matchless as they have always been, and it can still teach self reliance and co-operation in equal and balanced measure.

2 The Modern Gliding Club

THE BGA AND EUROPE

The function of the UK's CAA (Civil Aviation Authority) was to ensure that aviation in this country was both safe and legal, two requirements which are not always the same thing. As part of European Integration, the CAA will continue to attempt to perform the perfect balancing act between the letter of the law and common sense, but now as a 'competent authority' under the European Air Safety Agency (EASA), who will be creating the regulations and who answer only to the European parliament. A predictable result has been additional layers of 'administration', and the dreary inevitability with which prices have increased and paperwork has proliferated. Although EASA has the final say in all matters aeronautical, the British Gliding Association (BGA), via the CAA, remains responsible for the conduct and practices of gliding in the UK. The CAA will continue to enjoy many of its previous powers, which have included the ability to bring any aviation activity to a complete standstill if they deem it necessary, and the authority to treat regulatory non-compliance as a criminal offence.

It is rather unfortunate that the aviation branch with the highest public profile, though not the most central by any means, is the Air Accidents Investigation Branch (AAIB). This is largely because aviation accidents can infrequently involve headline-grabbing numbers of deaths. Sadly, the real shock horror which we tolerate with misplaced equanimity as just another of those 'unavoidable things', is car accidents, which kill far more of us in smaller, less dramatic but far more frequent accidents.

The clubs' relationship to the BGA

The BGA itself is not a governing body as such, but a co-ordinator of gliding activities and standards in this country, and the members of its main committee are voted in by the member clubs.

Gliding club organisation

Gliding clubs vary widely in what they are able to provide the budding pilot – not necessarily in terms of instruction, but in the facilities that they offer and the numbers of days on which they operate. Because gliding is almost entirely run by people who actively participate in the sport, at whatever level, it is controlled largely by enthusiasts, the overwhelming majority of whom provide their services for free. The drawback of this situation is that not everyone has time free when it suits the club, so the number of club members can be the determining factor in a few key areas. For example, some of the smaller clubs only operate at weekends, or at weekends and maybe on one or two other days during the week. The larger, commercially run clubs, on the other hand, are invariably seven day a week operations, usually but not always throughout the year.

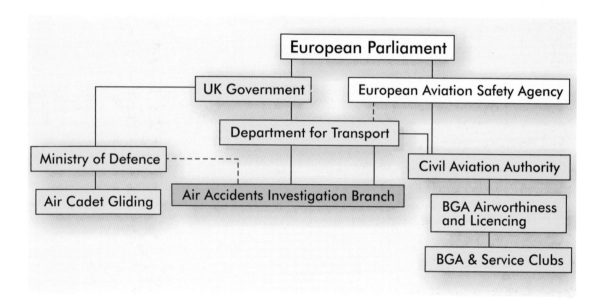

EASA, CAA and BGA.

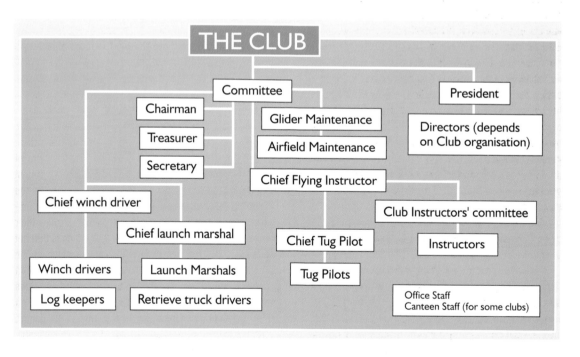

Typical club structure.

Ground facilities can vary hugely, but don't judge the worth of a club from that. In terms of broadening your gliding experience, some of the most interesting and instructive sites from which to fly don't have bunkhouses, restaurant facilities or enormously plush clubhouses and well stocked bars. They probably all have toilets. The composition of club-owned fleets can also vary and be anything from all old to all new. As far as learning to glide is concerned such differences are largely cosmetic, but the fleet's composition can influence the costs, with more modern fleets being more expensive. The majority of the clubs that offer to train you will have at least two dual-seat training gliders, plus several club owned single-seat gliders to which you will convert when you go solo.

Once you have passed beyond the very early ab initio (under instruction) stage, and particularly once you are solo, most clubs will expect you to help out in some way. Depending on your experience and how the club is organised, you might be asked to help out at the launch point in some capacity, or train to be a winch driver, a cable retrieve truck driver or to do some other necessary job suited better to your particular skills. No gliding club can function without someone doing these often mundane jobs.

Gliding can take up quite a bit of time, and though, generally speaking, there is no need for you to be on a gliding field the entire day, it is appreciated if you do more than just take your flights. For example, you might turn up at the beginning of the day and help get operations started by moving the gliders from the hangar to the launch point, under the supervision of the duty instructor. Nobody would be too worried if you left after lunch. Likewise, if you arrived at lunchtime it would be appreciated if you stayed until the end of flying and helped put everything away. None of this is obligatory, of course, but people who never seem to be around when there's work to do, yet suddenly spring into existence when it's their turn to fly, are not popular. There's nothing particularly personal about this. Cooperation and 'making your contribution' is vital to the health of gliding clubs, of whatever size, and even if your own efforts earn you no big pats on the back nor any universal acclaim, most clubs simply can't get by without it.

COSTS

What you get for your money and how costs and 'services' vary from club to club.

If you take up gliding, it is not possible to say exactly what the costs will be. They vary from club to club, often markedly, and the costs related to the actual flying will depend to some extent on your ability. Though on the whole cheaper than power flying, gliding is more expensive in terms of time. Many clubs are gradually evolving strategies to cope with the large changes in people's lifestyles that the technological revolution has brought about. Nevertheless, whatever the club's strategy, there is a training syllabus which must be completed and cannot be skipped over.

On joining a club you will pay an annual membership fee which is there to cover, either wholly or partially, the club's fixed costs such as insurance, rates and so on. Clubs may use some of their annual flying income to cover some portion of these fixed costs, but such income does depend very much on the weather behaving itself. You can also be charged a one-off joining fee whose raison d'etre is obscure, but many sporting organisations (eg golf clubs) levy them. Subsequently you will pay for each launch and for the flying time, but not for any flying instruction you receive thereafter – that will be free. Most clubs use winching and aerotowing for launching, with a few offering either aerotowing or winching only. Each method of launching has its pros and cons.

University gliding clubs and cadet schemes

A number of universities in this country have their own gliding clubs, usually run in conjunction with a civilian or occasionally a service gliding club, which provides them with launching facilities and, occasionally, gliders. There are almost always concessionary rates in the clubs for students in full-time education, regardless of whether the local university either has an official gliding club of its own, or any gliding equipment.

Many clubs run cadet schemes for people between the ages of about fourteen and twenty, again providing concessionary rates but sometimes requiring that the flying time

A typical GRP (glass reinforced plastic) club glider fleet, with launch and support vehicles.

is partly paid for by 'work in kind'. This might involve doing some unpaid job on a fairly regular basis (log keeping, say) for the club. If you fall into any of the categories just mentioned, speak to the local club and find out if they have any 'schemes' and if so, what the terms are – they vary. In any case, the BGA is interested in getting more and younger people into gliding.

Instructors and the training process

The overwhelming majority of club instructors have come up through the ranks at their club. Most are unpaid non-professional instructors who do it because they like gliding and instructing. For any club member to become any kind of instructor they need the approval of the club's Chief Flying Instructor (CFI), the majority support of the club's other instructors, permission from the club committee (depending on the club's rules and regulations), and must have already shown themselves to be helpful club members and responsible pilots.

There are several grades of instructor. The first is the Basic Instructor (BI), usually trained by the club, and allowed to give very limited instruction above a specified minimum height (500ft) during the Trial Instructional Flights, which almost every club provides to interested members of the public. BIs are supervised by instructors of higher grades.

The second category is the Assistant Instructor. These pilots have been on an instructor's course run by the BGA's National Coach and his/her deputies. These week long courses ensure standardization, teach the candidates how to instruct every exercise in detail, what to teach and when, as well as stretching and improving their skills and judgement. These courses are hard work, and so they should be. Anyone who doesn't reach a certain minimum standard is not accepted as an Assistant Instructor.

The next stage is the Fully Rated Instructor who is supposed to know everything and is, like the CFI, responsible for everyone. Luckily, controlling the weather isn't part of the job description. Apart from demonstrating breadth of knowledge and experience, the rating's only other advantage, and a dubious one in the view of many instructors, is that once you have it you can be chosen to be the CFI. The club and the BGA have to agree on your appointment as CFI, and it is within the BGA's remit to refuse a candidate the required CFI Endorsement to their rating record. The CFI's job is not for the naive.

There are other instructing levels, largely to do with organisation and the setting and maintaining of standards, such as Regional Examiners, Senior Regional Examiners, and so on. Instructing matters in general are overseen by the BGA's Instructors Committee.

Most clubs operate an instructing rota of some kind, so that there are always instructors on duty at the weekends, or whenever the club operates. This is very likely to mean that you won't always fly with the same instructor. There are varying views on how efficient this is from the trainee's point of view, particularly since each first flight with a previously unknown instructor can be more of a social than an instructional occasion, with the trainee and instructor sizing each other up. It is very important that you should have confidence in your instructor(s), and yet, from instructing experience, it is surprisingly easy for trainees to act as if they were entirely alone in the two-seater glider. If it's any consolation, the instructor has no more desire than you to be hurt.

You may find that you don't hit it off with some instructors – it happens. You may also feel that you would get more consistency by staying with the same instructor(s), and many clubs run evening flying sessions during the summer, and/or courses during the week, all of which help to address that particular problem. On the other hand, being taught by several different instructors does have the advantage of exposing you to a greater range of opinions and advice, which is useful.

ABOUT LEARNING

The speed with which we pick up new skills varies, but learning new ones requires plenty of repetition, and the older we are, the more is needed. There is also a significant difference between remembering stuff and then going through the motions, and really understanding what that 'stuff' is about.

We all vary in how quickly we assimilate new information and how much and how accurately we remember any of it, so quoting average times (as this book does in a few places) can be misleading. For example, were we asked to rate ourselves as drivers, almost every one of us would modestly admit to being rather better than average, which can't actually be true! Some are better, some are worse, and regardless of what 'average' might suggest, very few people actually are 'average'. In terms of learning something new, therefore, you won't really know how long it takes until after you've learnt it.

That aside, our comprehension, recall and execution are likely to be poor if the new subject is one that also rouses anxiety, and unfortunately flying can be rather good at that. In any case, in the initial stages of learning to fly what we remember of a short briefing will probably be three things,

at the most, and none of them may have much relevance to what we're about to do, or even, occasionally, what was actually said. For instance, the three things might be: (1) I didn't understand a word of any of that, (2) there was a mention of 'attitude' (what has my behaviour got to do with flying an aeroplane?), and (3) the instructor said 'Don't do this', but what was it?

As your skills improve apparently unrelated bits of advice and practice will fit together, and at some point you will realize that you can do an action and monitor it at the same time without having to exhaust every mental resource in the process. You also remember more of what you've been told.

DEALING WITH ANXIETY

There is an old quip to the effect that if you aren't scared then you haven't really grasped the seriousness of the situation. Some of us can swim if we fall out of a boat, but none of us can fly if we fall out of an aeroplane. Flight can also cause some very peculiar and occasionally not very pleasant sensations, and for all its wonders, it speaks directly to primitive and not entirely irrational fears. What, we ask, is holding us up? Will we suddenly fall and be broken? In small doses anxiety can increase alertness – that's one of its functions – but too much of it leads to paralysis. We either hold our breath or it becomes very fast and shallow (hyper-ventilation). Both alter the oxygen/carbon dioxide balance in the blood and lead to a sense of unfocused physical unease. As a result we feel even more anxious and even less inclined to breathe normally. If this continues for long enough, our vision fades away and shortly afterwards we pass out. Telling people to relax is a bit like saying 'be spontaneous', so without becoming completely obsessed by your breathing – which will lead to other problems – try to keep it near normal. This disrupts the loop described and should help you relax. Your brain will appreciate the increase in oxygen and work a great deal better as a result.

One symptom of anxiety and tension is indirect and usually goes unnoticed because we are already a bit preoccupied. Let's say that you are flying the glider during one of your first winch launches. For some reason the rudder – the control operated by your feet – seems much heavier and harder to move than usual. Is the instructor surreptitiuously interfering with the controls? If you believe this to be the case at any time during your training, say so. You won't learn anything useful if you are being secretly assisted in your efforts, particularly by someone who said that they had handed control over to you. The much more likely cause of the heaviness is that you are bracing your feet against the rudder bar/pedals, and are, in effect, working against yourself. Relaxing and pushing with one foot at a time works wonders.

Understanding how aeroplanes work can also help. If nothing else, it will tell you what can realistically go wrong, and can give you some useful clue to putting it right.

IN THE BEGINNING

A question asked occasionally by prospective pilots is 'Will I be sent off on my own?', by which they mean straight-away, on their first ever flight. If you've never flown before, you will not be sent solo until you've done the required amount of dual training first.

However, in the early days solo training was standard, and done in gliders that were little more than a broomstick dangling under wings that looked like a spare set of garage doors. The first lessons were about how to use the controls to keep the wings level, and were often catapult-launched ground slides. If a winch or tow-car were used the instructor might run or cycle alongside the glider, shouting advice. At this very early stage you would never leave the ground, except by accident. Once you had mastered keeping the wings level you'd be briefed on the use of the other controls, and then the winch or tow-car driver – who had a lot of influence on how the flight proceeded – would give the glider slightly more airspeed so that you could become airborne, if only for a few wobbly seconds. Eventually you would be given a high launch and told to 'do a circuit'. Given that the performance of such gliders was what you'd expect from garage doors, arriving back where you started wasn't always easy.

The crash rate was high, but the accidents occurred usually at such low speeds that people weren't often badly hurt. Solo training worked, after a fashion – many excellent pilots went through it – but the crack of rending sticks and the ping of snapping rigging wires were the sounds of the flying operation coming to a full stop. If nothing else, the economic arguments against solo training were very strong. The first two-seat training gliders appeared before

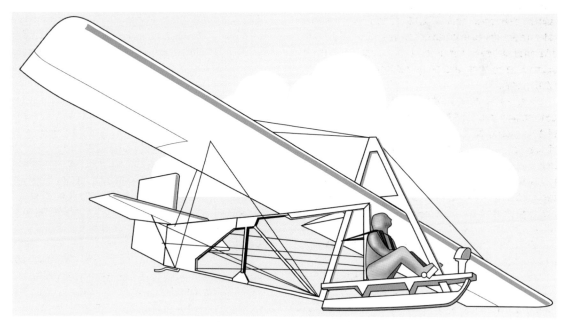

Solo training glider: Grunau.

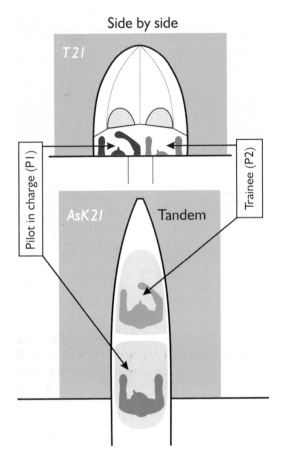

Seating positions.

World War II, in the 1930s, but it took until the 1960s before solo training was everywhere replaced by purpose-built two-seaters, either tandem – one seat ahead of the other – or side by side (see above). Dual training is excellent news for today's trainees (and their clubs) because even though modern gliders are far stronger and generally more agreeable to fly than yesteryear's 'open plan' solo trainers, they are also much heavier and faster. Attempting to solo train anyone in today's super ships would be little more than an invitation to have a serious accident.

An important feature of almost every two-seater training glider, with the occasional eccentric exception which you aren't very likely to come across, is the duplication of the controls, if not always the instruments. For example, in the two-seater positions illustrated above, the tandem set-up has a complete set of inter-linked controls in both the front and back seats, as well as duplicated instrument panels. The panels will usually have an identical layout, so that when the instructor refers to an instrument at the top right of either panel it will be the same one. The side by seat arrangement will in general only duplicate the controls, one set on the left and another on the right, and there will only be one instrument panel.

YOUR VERY FIRST FLIGHT

Your first flight is an important one, and it will begin before you get anywhere near a glider. Gliding sites can look completely innocuous – glider parked over here, group of people away over there, large inviting areas of grass on which to lounge and have a picnic – but whatever it looks like, there are a few things you simply mustn't do when you're there. Even if you received an explanatory leaflet beforehand, whether through the post or downloaded from the Internet, when you arrive on the airfield you will either be given a direct briefing by an instructor, or shown a short video presentation about how to keep out of trouble. Take good note of what is said. Before you fly you are also likely to be given a guided tour of a glider, and regaled with a brief non-technical explanation of how it works.

Once you've been escorted out to the launch point, and before you even get your feet into the glider, you may well be told how to bail out of it! This may take you aback, but don't be put off. The chances of you ever having to use a parachute are minute, but in that very unlikely event it would be greatly to your advantage if you knew exactly what to do, so if you are going to wear one you will first be given some help to put it on, and then receive brief instruction on its use (Chapter 8 gives more detail about this). Parachutes are fairly heavy and rather unwieldy. They are also designed to be relatively easy to deploy, and it's not difficult to do this by accident, which is why you get advice and assistance when you put it on and when you take it off.

Getting into a glider can be awkward. Cockpits have high sides and the seat pan can be a close fit even for standard-size people, but once you're in the seat and reasonably comfortable, someone will help you strap in. The one thing you don't want to feel or be is 'loose' in the cockpit, so the straps are done up quite tightly.

Cloudscape. On your own.

The instructor will have told you what to expect of the launch, what will be demonstrated, when you will be able to 'have a go' – you don't have to if you don't want to – and the vital form of words which should be used when control is handed over to you, or you hand it back. A series of pre-launch checks are then done before the launch cable is hooked on. A glider doesn't have the same kind of 'one wheel (or more) on each side' arrangement of powered aeroplanes, so a wingtip holder is needed to keep the wings level at the start of the take-off run. While the view forwards and to each side is exceptionally good in gliders, the view directly backwards is restricted. Before the launch can take place someone outside the glider – who may be the wingtip holder – has to check that other aircraft or ground vehicles aren't going to conflict with it in any way. Quite often – it depends on the club's launch-point set-up – the person who gives the vital 'all clear above and behind' may also be the person who communicates with the launch vehicle, or, if you are exceptionally lucky, the team working the bungee rope for a catapult launch from a hill (for more detail of this unusual method of launch, see the end of Chapter 4). As you sit there wondering what to expect next, the tug, winch or tow-car is instructed to 'take up slack' and very gradually the cable or rope lying ahead of you on the ground will go tight. At this point the 'all out' signal is

given and away you go. Aerotowing is fairly sedate, and the initial acceleration quite modest. If the wind is light the wingtip holder may run quite a long way before letting go. The chances are that your first launch will be by winch, possibly auto-tow (both are referred to as 'wire launches'), which can, by comparison with aerotowing, seem a bit alarming, or very exciting, or both, depending on your temperament. With winching in particular the wingtip holder usually lets go almost immediately, which gives you some idea of the robustness of the acceleration. In practice this means that it can take tens of seconds for an aerotowed glider to reach flying speed, with the glider usually taking off well before the tow plane. On a winch launch the glider will reach take-off speed (approximately 50mph) within a few seconds. With any launch the ground run can be a bit bumpy, depending on the surface you're taking off from, and can also be quite noisy, but at some point the bumping will stop suddenly, things will get quieter, and even though you may only be a whisker clear of the ground, now you are flying.

Aerotowing is about doggedly following the towplane, or tug. The glider can't climb any more quickly than the tug, so a launch to 2,000ft will take as long as it takes the tug to get there, which can be several minutes. Wire launching is different. You probably won't reach 2,000ft, but you'll get

Single seat glider being aerotowed launched. The same 'support, run, let go' technique is used for all launches.

to the top of the launch a lot more quickly. The initial climb is quite shallow, but not the rest of it. Most of the launch will seem to happen with astonishing speed even though it's not in fact all that quick – it takes approximately one and a half minutes from start to release. There will only be clouds and sky to see ahead of you during the climb, so look out sideways to see just how steep it is – but having noted that and probably swallowed rather hard, look beyond at the unfolding view.

Release from aerotow is straightforward. The instructor has a good look round to make sure it is safe to go, releases the tow cable, and then pulls up into a gentle turn to clear the end of the rope. The tow-plane then dives away, back to the airfield. At the top of a winch or auto-tow launch, when the glider is more or less level and won't climb any higher, the instructor either lowers the nose slightly and releases the launch cable, or the automatic safety device built into the release hook 'back releases' the cable and does the job for him. Whenever and however the cable is released there can be a sudden loud 'clunk!' which instructors are so used to that they can forget to mention it

beforehand. If your first flight is in a metal glider the release of the cable can sound like a pistol shot.

What may come as a surprise both during the launch and after release is how noisy gliders can be, though some are much noisier than others. If you've travelled in a commercial airliner the background roar that you hear is a mix of engine and airflow noise. In a glider the 'gravity engine' (see next chapter), which is effectively running the show, is silent, but you will hear the hiss of the airflow. During a winch launch you might also hear random clunks and thumps. The instructor may have explained beforehand that occasionally launch cables break, and some of the noises you hear will be due to previous cable repairs, when a hydraulic press is used to squeeze a small metal collar round the two overlapping broken ends. When the collars run through the winch rollers that guide the cable on to the winch cable drum, there is a clunk and occasionally a jerk. The launch cable is taut as you climb, and any noises transmitted along it from the winch are magnified by the glider which, being largely hollow, acts like a sounding box.

Pretending to be a fighter pilot. J. ROBSON

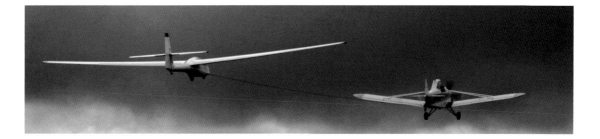

Puchacz two-seat glider on tow behind a Pawnee. J. BRIDGE

Talk about winch-cable breaks may fill you with trepidation, but you need to be warned about them because the standard procedure for most breaks is for the pilot to lower the glider's nose rather smartly. The result feels like going over a hump-backed bridge a bit too fast, and is one good reason for having tight straps. It's best to be forewarned about the possibility of breaks and the way they are dealt with, if only so that you don't get taken completely by surprise. In any case, slightly unpleasant sensation though it can be, it is infinitely preferable to the pilot doing nothing.

Once the cable is released the glider will become quieter, and you and your instructor will be able to converse in normal voices. You will be asked to help with the lookout, spotting where other aircraft are, and so on. What follows next depends on what you want to do. Some people find the view utterly entrancing and are quite happy looking at that – if the weather is particularly clear you can see thirty or more miles without any trouble. On the other hand, rather than look at the view, you might like to have a go at flying the glider. The instructor will first demonstrate how its speed and direction are controlled, and you will be asked to follow through with your hands lightly on the controls. Then control is handed over to you.

You'll probably be a bit nervous, and feeling as if you are sitting on a billiard ball balanced on the top of a pin – a precarious position from which you might think you can only fall! The good news is that most two-seat gliders are designed to be easy to fly and one result is that they can keep bowling steadily along, if not forever, at least for several minutes without anyone needing to touch the controls at all. This is very helpful, because when you are given the controls it means that you don't have to be constantly 'doing something' with them. A big chunk of

'learning how to fly' is about leaving the aeroplane alone when it's doing all right. In any case, now's your chance to see what happens when you 'do things'. As demonstrated, ease the stick forwards a small amount and the nose lowers. Ease the stick back and the nose comes up again. Experiment. Try not to be jerky and robotic with the controls, but don't be too coy, either. The glider responds more quickly to fore-and-aft movement of the stick than it does to the side-to-side movement required to tilt (bank) it and make it turn. Be easy with the fore-and-aft movement, but if you aren't positive enough with the side-to-side movement nothing much will happen and the diameter of the resulting turn will take up most of the country. Using all the controls together correctly can be challenging initially, so it is usual for the instructor to operate the rudder for you (that's what your feet would normally be doing) while you move the stick.

Eventually the glider will have descended to a point where you must start the circuit to land. The 'circuit' is a pattern, rather like a race-track in the sky, that aircraft follow when they're preparing to land. If you have been doing the flying so far the instructor may talk you round the circuit until you are abeam the landing area, and at that point will take over control and do the rest.

When a glider is approaching to land it will usually be flown slightly faster than during the rest of the flight, launch excluded. The reason for this is largely to do with the speed of the wind, as described in a later chapter. In any case, if the wind is at all strong you will not only be going quite fast prior to landing – though it may not look that way – but also pointing fairly steeply at the ground. The instructor will use the airbrakes – there will be another 'clunk' as he opens them – to control the rate of descent. The noise level will increase. When quite close to the

In the alps. J. BRIDGE

ground the instructor will raise the nose of the glider so that it stays flying a few inches above the ground. The speed will then gradually wash away, and once the glider has touched down you will be subjected to the same kind of bumping and noise that you were on the take-off run. When the glider comes to a halt, one wing will go down on to the ground: this is rather inelegant given how 'flowing' most flight is, but unavoidable. You will be helped out of the cockpit, and given assistance removing the parachute.

Hopefully your first flight will have been very enjoyable, and you will have a sense of the magic that attracts so many people to gliding.

3 How Gliders Work

BASIC LAYOUT

The basic layout of gliders is common to most aircraft. The major structural components are the wing, which provides the major force required to keep the glider airborne; the fuselage, which is a place to put the cockpit and the pilot; and the fin and tailplane, both of which attach to the fuselage and are aids to stability. The hinged surfaces, which provide the pilot with the necessary control, are the ailerons on the wings, the rudder attached to the fin and the elevator attached to the tailplane. The airbrakes are used largely to control the rate of descent during the approach and landing. We'll be looking in more detail at each of the controls and what they do later.

You are going to be chucked in at the deep end at this point, because here comes some of the theory. There is no need for anyone in the initial stages of learning to fly to know very much about how gliders work, and most of it won't make much sense until you have done at least some of the training. Rather than split out the various theoretical bits over the course of this book, they have been gathered here in one chapter for easier reference. By all means skip anything you don't understand, but come back to it later.

To start with we'll be talking only about powered aeroplanes because, though gliders work in almost exactly the same way, the fact that they don't seem to have an engine adds a slight complication which is best described after looking at simpler set-ups.

HOW WINGS CREATE LIFT

When you pick something like a book off the floor, you must make an effort to lift it up. If you let go, the book drops back to the floor. Aircraft have much the same problem and need something to lift them up and then keep them there. For conventional aeroplanes the key to creating the required lifting/supporting force is the wing's cross sectional shape, its aerofoil. One aero-dynamicist, when asked why aerofoils worked at all, replied 'it's magic'. He wasn't being entirely frivolous. An aerofoil is basically little more than a flat plate bent into a curve, yet when air flows over it some very odd and rather surprising effects occur.

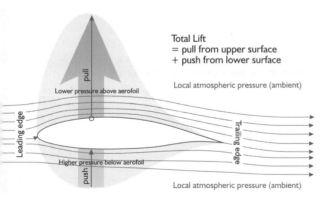

Total Lift
= pull from upper surface
+ push from lower surface

Local atmospheric pressure (ambient)

pull

Lower pressure above aerofoil

Leading edge

Trailing edge

Higher pressure below aerofoil

push

Local atmospheric pressure (ambient)

Airflow streamlines over an aerofoil.

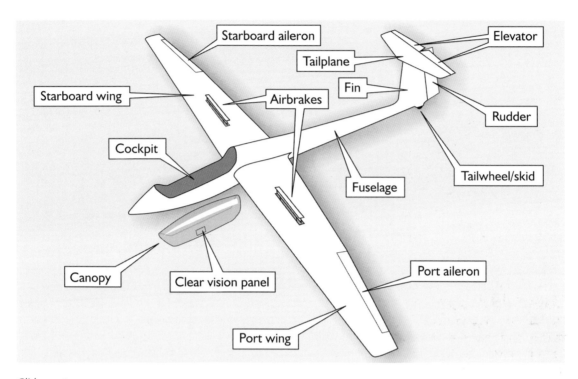

Glider parts.

In normal flight a wing will sit slightly nose up in relation to the airflow. Air that goes beneath the wing is pushed downwards out of the way, creating an upward force – you can think of the undersurface as operating something like a water ski. Rather unexpectedly, it is the upper surface which normally creates the major part of the total lift, and how it does so is much more complicated.

The curvature of the upper surface – in particular the shape of the leading edge – causes the top surface airflow to accelerate, and this leads to a drop in its pressure. In combination with some other effects, upper surface lift is a result of the lowered pressure and a reaction to the pressure-assisted bending of the airflow stream to follow the aerofoil's shape. This same combination also helps keeps the air smooth and 'attached' for longer than would otherwise be the case – but even so, at some point the upper surface airflow will begin to slow down and its pressure start returning to 'normal' – that is, back to the local (ambient) pressure. At about this point the airflow stream, in effect, trips over itself and becomes increasingly turbulent. Exactly when and where this happens, and how it affects the total lift, depends on factors that we'll look at in a moment.

A wing's total lift is therefore the sum of an effective upward 'pull' from the aerofoil's upper surface and an upward 'push' from its underside.

SPEED AND ANGLE OF ATTACK

The actual strength of the lifting force depends on the area of the wing, the exact shape of the aerofoil and, far more importantly – at least from the pilot's point of view – the speed of the airflow and the angle at which it approaches the aerofoil (known as the Angle of Attack, or AoA – pronounced, tele-tubby like, as Eh Oh Eh).

The AoA is defined as the angle between the aerofoil chord line and the relative airflow. The chord line is a straight line joining the nose and tail of the aerofoil. The relative airflow is in the opposite direction to the aircraft's flight path, and the flight path is the direction in which the

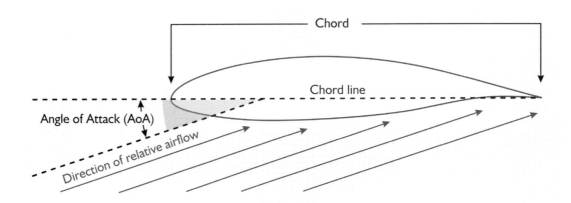

Relative airflow and the angle of attack.

aircraft is actually moving, which may have nothing to do with the direction in which it happens to be pointing.

The relationship between speed and AoA is pretty straightforward. In steady, straight and level flight, if the speed is high then (all other things being equal) the angle at which the airflow meets the aerofoil will be small. If the aircraft is flying very slowly, then the airflow speed will also be low, but the angle at which the air is striking the wing will be large. There are limits to just how large the AoA can be, as we'll see later, but the force supporting the aeroplane is a mixture of lift created by the speed of the airflow and lift created by the angle at which the airflow approaches the wing, the AoA.

As an aside, it is probably worth noting that though it is conventional to talk of the airflow as moving over an aerofoil, it is almost invariably the movement of the aeroplane through the air which creates that flow. What matters most is the flow, not how it is created. The conventional viewpoint of stationary aerofoil, moving air, has its roots in wind tunnel experiments, and very likely the convenience of illustrators. In airflow diagrams the air usually has all the arrows!

LIFT AND WEIGHT, THRUST AND DRAG

It is an unfortunate fact of physics that the very act of doing almost anything produces the majority of forces trying to prevent it, and that is certainly true of flight.

For an aircraft to maintain level flight, the lift (which is usually referred to simply as L) must be equal and opposite to the weight (W). If L is less than W then the aircraft won't take-off or, if airborne, it will gradually descend. Likewise, if L is greater than W then the aircraft will climb.

For conventional aeroplanes the main purpose of the engine is to pull or push them along fast enough for their wings to be able to produce the necessary lift. Unfortunately, the moment the aeroplane begins to roll along the runway for take-off, its progress is hindered by a number of forces, one of which is air resistance. Air resistance, or aerodynamic drag (usually referred to simply as drag or just D), increases with speed and is governed by what's known as a square law; so that if, say, the aeroplane goes three times as fast, the amount of drag will increase by nine times (3x3). The engine can only produce so much power (T for thrust), so even with the throttle fully open, there will be a speed where the drag and thrust components exactly balance each other (D=T), and the aeroplane won't go any faster. If this balance were to be achieved during the take-off run, then the aeroplane would never take-off.

A glider has no engine in the conventional sense of the word, but it does have mass and weight and is just as much at the mercy of aerodynamic drag as any other aeroplane. For exactly the same reasons that an aeroplane needs an engine to move it along, so too does a glider, and its engine is gravity. Unlike all other engines gravity is both 100 per cent reliable and 100 per cent consistent, but it does have some drawbacks. It always works in exactly the same direction, downwards, and doesn't come equipped with a throttle or accelerator.

The simplest way to look at how gravity provides the glider with an engine is to compare it with what happens to something like a skateboard, for example, when it is first on level ground, and then on a hill. If you set the board down on level ground it will just sit there and go nowhere. The only way you can make it move is for you to act as the engine and push it along, or you look for a suitable hill and freewheel down it.

The skateboard rolls down the hill because a component of the board and the rider's weight is in effect acting along the hill – probably clearer if you look at the diagram opposite. You can think of this as being thrust (T) because it has exactly the same effect as an engine. The speed of the skateboard is related to the steepness of the hill. Steeper means faster. What you might expect, perhaps, is that if you start freewheeling down a steadily sloping hill you will just keep on going faster and faster for as long as the hill lasts, but that isn't what happens. As with the earlier example, at some point the T and D forces will balance out and the board won't go any faster.

This is more or less exactly how a glider operates. However, having located the 'engine', there is one other question that needs asking. What would have happened to the skateboard if the ground hadn't been there? With no support it would have fallen straight down. For the descent to be angled there must be a surface of some sort against which the skateboard's weight can act, and that surface is the sloping ground. For conventional aircraft like gliders, the equivalent surface is an invisible one created by the lift from the wings.

Gliders enter chicken and egg territory here. If the airflow over the wings is to be sufficient to provide the required lifting force, the glider must move forward through the air, but in free flight the only way it can do so is by rolling downhill. The first consequence is that the lift force is tilted in the direction of flight and so won't quite support the weight. In fact, a glider's weight is supported by a combination of lift and drag, known as the Total Reaction (TR). The second consequence is that since a glider launched into completely still air must gradually and inevitably descend, the length of any flight would appear to be determined entirely by the height of the launch – gliding as aerial tobogganing. Luckily, nature has some clever tricks up her sleeve, and, as we'll see in a later chapter, rising air completely alters that limited picture.

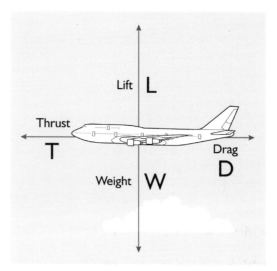

Lift, drag, weight and thrust.

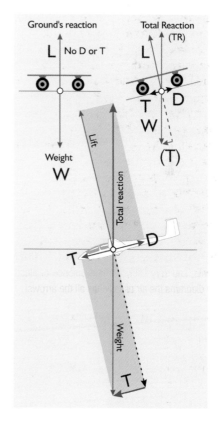

Skateboard and glider.

THE STALL

In any given set of circumstances a wing will only be able to provide so much lift and no more. As previously described, the amount of lift an aerofoil generates depends on a combination of AoA and speed-generated lift. When an aeroplane slows down the speed-generated component of the total lift being produced by the wing decreases, but if the aircraft is to stay at the same height the weight still has to be supported. The lift shortfall, so to speak, can only be made up by an increase in the wing's AoA. At some point, when the AoA reaches a high enough angle (the critical or stalling angle), the air flowing over the majority of the aerofoil's upper surface finds it impossible to hang on any longer and swirls chaotically away towards the trailing edge. The wing has stalled. It is not true that at this point the wing simply stops working; it is just that you can't get any more lift out of it, and if the AoA increases any further the lift will decrease, often quite sharply. The stalling exercises in Chapter 9 describe what happens next.

What is a load and how does it relate to stalling?

By sitting on a chair you subject it to a load, and no doubt if the chair could talk it would tell you exactly how much. A load cannot exist by itself because it is the reaction of a material (wood in this case) to an applied force (your weight). If the load is too great the chair breaks. Most chairs are designed to take a large range of weights without either breaking or becoming permanently distorted, though all will bend, albeit to a minute degree, when sat upon. The same goes for aircraft structures.

Aircraft are subjected to many different kinds of forces and varying loads, most of which are the result of acceleration. This isn't acceleration in the 'going faster' sense that we usually think of it, but acceleration brought about by changes in direction. If you whirl a stone on a piece of string you can feel a force in the string, which gets larger and larger the faster you whirl the stone around. If you suddenly release the string the stone (viewed from above)

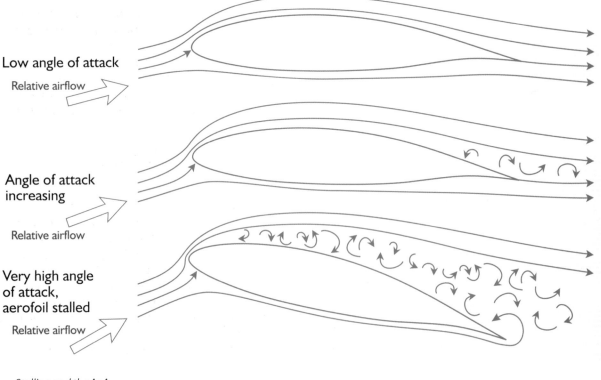

Low angle of attack

Relative airflow

Angle of attack increasing

Relative airflow

Very high angle of attack, aerofoil stalled

Relative airflow

Stalling and the AoA.

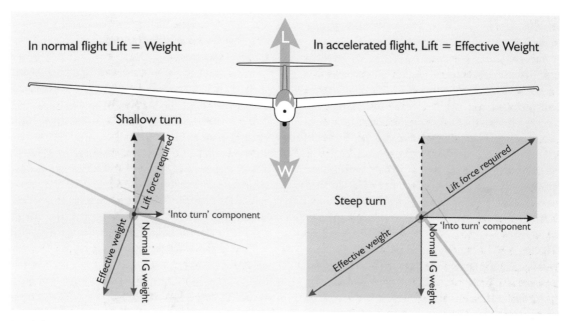

In normal flight Lift = Weight

In accelerated flight, Lift = Effective Weight

Shallow turn

Lift force required

'Into turn' component

Effective weight

Normal 1G weight

Steep turn

Lift force required

'Into turn' component

Effective weight

Normal 1G weight

Loads in a turn.

immediately shoots off in a straight line. Much the same applies to getting anything to go round a corner. The change requires a 'make-it-so' force in the intended direction, and the quicker you want the change to occur the greater the force that's needed.

One result is that as a glider manoeuvres the pilot will feel heavier or lighter. These changes in 'effective weight' (i.e. anything more or less than normal) are measured in terms of G. 1G is the normal force of gravity, so if the pilot feels twice as heavy as normal, then his or her effective weight has doubled and he or she is being subjected to a load of 2G. Four times as heavy would be 4G. If the pilot can feel these loads, then the glider's effective weight has to be increasing, and to counterbalance this the wing must produce more lift. For example, in straight and level flight the lift near enough equals the weight (L=W), but any manoeuvre that increases the effective weight by, say, three times, will require three times as much support (ie 3xL=3xW), and this must be provided either by an increase in speed, or AoA, or both. Thus, if the speed stays constant during a manoeuvre that results in G (and therefore the effective weight) becoming greater than 1, the wing can only produce the extra lift by an increase in the AoA. If that reaches the critical angle during all of this,

the wing will stall. The practical result is that if you subject the aircraft to a sufficiently high load, or pull enough G, you can stall at any speed.

Your training as a glider pilot will cover stalling in some detail, concentrating on the symptoms of an approaching stall, how to avoid stalling accidentally, what happens if you do, and how to recover – which, encouragingly, is straightforward.

CONTROL IN THREE DIMENSIONS

Even though cars can go up and down hills, they are really only moving around in two dimensions. There is the backwards/ forwards dimension, which is controlled by the accelerator and the brakes (the decelerator), and the left/right dimension controlled by the steering wheel. The important point about these two dimensions is that for the driver to have any say in where the car goes, each dimension requires a separate control. Aircraft move in three dimensions – the extra dimension is up/down – and for a pilot, like the car driver, useful influence in all of them requires three controls. Ideally each control would affect only one dimension, but, for reasons about which

33

very little can be done, and which we will look at in a moment, this is virtually impossible.

The controls of a conventional aircraft consist of a hand-operated control column, usually referred to as the 'stick', and the foot operated 'rudder'. The stick controls both pitch and roll, and the rudder controls yaw, as described below. All the control surfaces form part of an aerofoil – whether that aerofoil is a vertical one, like the fin and rudder, or horizontal like the tailplane and elevator or the wing and the ailerons. They all work by changing the aerofoil's shape and the direction and strength of any force that it produces.

Pitch

Pitch is controlled by the elevator, which raises or lowers the glider's tail. Your instructor will refer often to 'the correct attitude', or just 'attitude', and this is how nose-up or nose-down the glider is in relation to the horizontal. Pitch changes affect both the glider's speed and the wing's

AoA. Strictly speaking, 'attitude' can refer to any position of an aircraft in relation to the horizontal plane, but in gliding it tends to refer specifically to pitch.

In terms of the skateboard analogy, the stick and elevator can be regarded as controlling the steepness of the hill down which the glider runs (see diagram on next page). To speed up you must ease the control stick forwards to lower the elevator, which then raises the tail and lowers the nose – steepening the slope. Conversely, to slow down you need to ease the stick back to raise the elevator, which then lowers the tail and raises the nose – making the slope less steep. There are very definite limits to how fast or slow you are able to go, and we'll look at these in slightly more detail later.

For a glider in free flight every attitude has a related speed. For example, if you are flying at 45kt the nose will be a certain distance below the horizon. If you then lower the glider's nose to the attitude normally associated with, for instance, 70kt, it will accelerate to 70kt. Likewise, if you then raise the nose back to the attitude associated

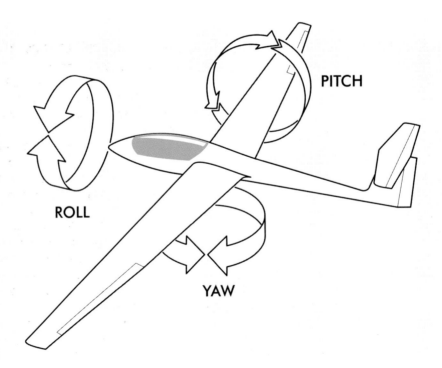

The aircraft axes.

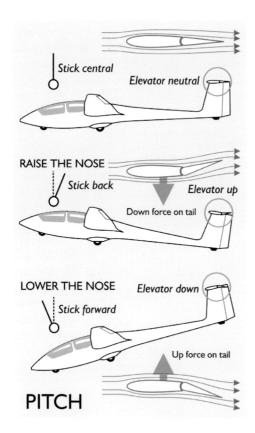

Stick central — Elevator neutral

RAISE THE NOSE — Stick back — Elevator up — Down force on tail

LOWER THE NOSE — Stick forward — Elevator down — Up force on tail

PITCH

Elevator and pitch.

with 45kt, the glider will decelerate to exactly that speed. This is one reason why your instructor will emphasize the importance of attitude. In mountainous areas cross checking the attitude with the air speed indicator (ASI) is very important because the hills can create false horizons.

Roll

The major requirement for going round any corner is creating the force needed to pull you in the direction in which you wish to go, and if you can't create that in one way or another you simply carry straight on. Rolling or banking the glider over to one side causes some of the wing's lifting force to act in the required direction, and it is this which pulls you round the corner. Roll is controlled by the ailerons. These operate differentially so that when one

goes up the other goes down. Moving the stick to the left, for example, raises the left aileron and lowers the right one. This decreases the lift from the left wing and increases it for the right wing, causing the glider to roll to the left. The bank angle is related to the rate of turn, ie how quickly you change direction. All other things being equal, steeper angles of bank result in faster rates of turn.

Yaw

Yaw is 'swing' in the horizontal plane and is controlled by the rudder. The rudder is used largely to counteract an unwanted effect created by the ailerons, and also to steer on the ground. If you want to yaw the glider to the right, you must push with your right foot. Even though yawing an airborne glider changes the direction in which the fuselage points, it will – depending on the speed – have little effect on the direction in which the glider is flying. Trying to turn when airborne using the rudder alone is incredibly inefficient, and can have some unexpected additional effects, as described below.

Primary and further (secondary) effects of the controls

A control's primary effects are those which the controls have been designed to produce and ideally would be the only ones, but there are further effects which you don't want but which you get anyway.

The elevator's primary effect is pitch and it has no others. The primary effect of the ailerons is to create roll, but a further effect is yaw. All other things being equal, lowering an aileron increases lift and drag on that side, while raising an aileron produces the opposite effect.

What is annoying about this is that because the ailerons operate differentially the drag effect works against the direction in which you wish to turn. For example, to turn right you must first roll to the right, so you move the stick in that direction. This raises the right aileron and reduces the lift and drag on that side. The left aileron meanwhile goes down, creating more lift and more drag on that side. If no other action is taken the glider will roll to the right, as you want, but initially the nose will yaw (swing) to the left. This effect is known as aileron drag or adverse yaw (see diagram on page 37).

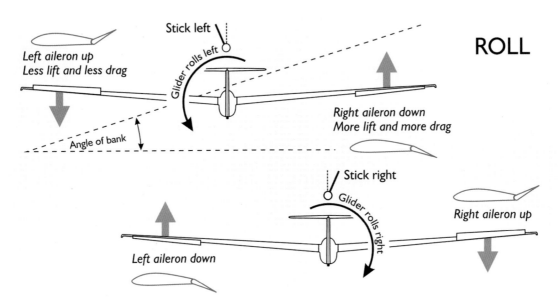

Ailerons and roll.

The primary effect of the rudder is yaw, but a further effect is roll. When the glider yaws one wing is swung forwards and speeded up, while the other is swung back and slowed down. This results in the forward-going wing developing more lift and the backward-going one developing less, causing the glider to roll towards the slower wing. The actual amount of roll that results from yaw depends, obviously, on the amount of rudder applied, but far more critically, on the speed of the glider.

If the glider is flying at a moderate speed, a large amount of rudder by itself will produce large amounts of yaw, but very small amounts of roll. The glider will swing, remain near enough wing level, and continue to fly on, but sideways. At very low speeds, close to the stall, use of the rudder by itself produces little yaw initially, but very large amounts of roll (see diagram on next page). It takes very little to spin in these circumstances – see the later notes on spinning.

Yaw has also an indirect effect on pitch. If you think of the yaw axis as being like a CD disc with the glider splayed across it, then as the glider banks the disc tilts. Applying rudder can then swing the nose above or below the horizon, altering the glider's attitude and thus having an effect on the speed. Equally, adverse yaw when the glider is banked can have the same effect. Any speed changes that result are not usually as large as one might expect because the glider is flying sideways and the flight path may not be quite what the attitude suggests.

Co-ordination

Very briefly, in gliders the rudder's main purpose is to overcome the adverse yaw created by the ailerons, and for balanced non-slipping or skidding flight, the two controls must be used together – hence co-ordination. Co-ordination is a difficult skill to acquire and can be a source of some frustration, so you will need, and get, plenty of practice at it – every time you fly.

Stick loads, control loads

Your instructor will almost certainly mention stick loads at some point, usually when talking about trimming (see later note). Stick loads (or forces) refer to the amount of effort you have to apply to the stick in order to manoeuvre the glider. Some gliders can be very 'heavy on the controls', and the stick loads are high. Others are 'light', so the stick forces may be very small. Elevator forces tend to be the lightest. The ailerons usually have the heaviest forces and are the most sluggish in response. Rudder loads can vary a great deal between types of glider.

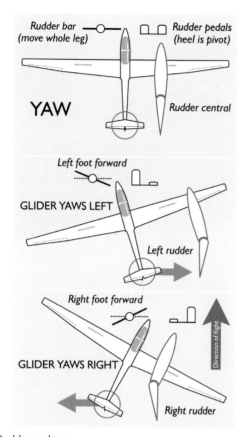

Rudder and yaw.

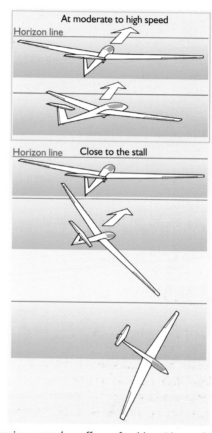

Changing secondary effects of rudder with speed.

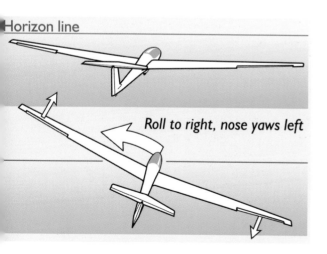

Ailerons and adverse yaw.

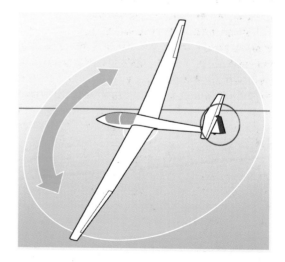

The effect of yaw on pitch.

4 Methods of Launch

WINCHING

Winching is probably the primary method of launch in the UK, but not every club provides it, either for reasons of space or because of local obstructions. Dropping a broken cable on power wires and shorting out entire villages is not a good move.

An evening winch launch.

The winch is sited at the upwind end of the take-off and landing strip (usually referred to as a 'run'). Most clubs use a truck to tow the winch cables to the launch point, where they are dropped. The truck returns to the winch, and after the cables have been 'used', picks them up from where they have landed, just ahead of the winch, and tows them back to the launch point again.

Description of winching

Attached to the glider end of the cable there is a parachute, a quick release hook which is attached to a weak link, a short wire strop and then a set of interlinked (Tost) rings. The exact sequence may differ from club to club, but the basics remain the same. The cable parachute provides drag and tension into the cable once the glider has released. This both prevents the cable falling in a tangled heap onto the ground and acts as a marker, allowing the cable to be drawn close to the winch for the tow truck to pick up (see diagram on next page). The set-up is such that during a launch the parachute collapses, and then deploys once the cable is released. The weak link is designed to break if the loads on the cable or the glider exceed certain levels, and prevents the glider from being over-stressed. How to fly the winch launch is described in more detail later.

The winch itself is a custom-built vehicle equipped with a powerful engine, with (usually) two rotating 'drums', one on each side. The stranded launch cable is wound onto the drums via a mechanical guide, which ensures that the cable is laid evenly. The winch driver controls the speed of the cable and, to a large degree, the speed of the launching glider.

Though many clubs use a tow truck or tractor to drag the cables from the winch to the launch point, some sites, where the terrain would make this a slow or difficult process, have a second and smaller retrieve winch at the launch point. The retrieve cable is much thinner than the main cable. A metal triangle joins the two cables together, with the free corner attached to the launch strop/weak link/Tost ring setup. Cable parachutes are not used in this case. The glider begins the launch to one side of the main cable, and after it has released at the top of the launch the retrieve winch is started up to pull the main cable back to the launch point (see diagram on next page).

Safety devices

There are several safety devices, the weak link in the cable being one of them – more about that in a later chapter. The hook used by the glider for winching has an automatic back release that will release the cable at the top of the launch if the pilot has forgotten to do so, and also when the cable is pulled backwards in relation to the glider – i.e. the glider is about to overfly the winch. The winch itself will be equipped with a weighted or spring-loaded guillotine to cut the cable in the very unlikely event of the glider being unable to release.

Auto-towing

Some clubs in the country, notably Lasham in Hampshire, have runways which are in good enough

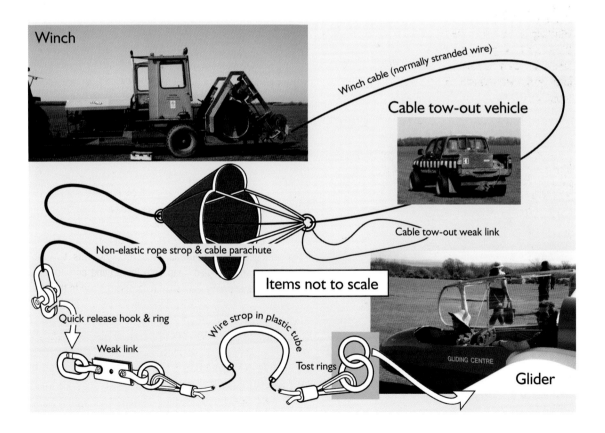

Winch set-up.

METHODS OF LAUNCH

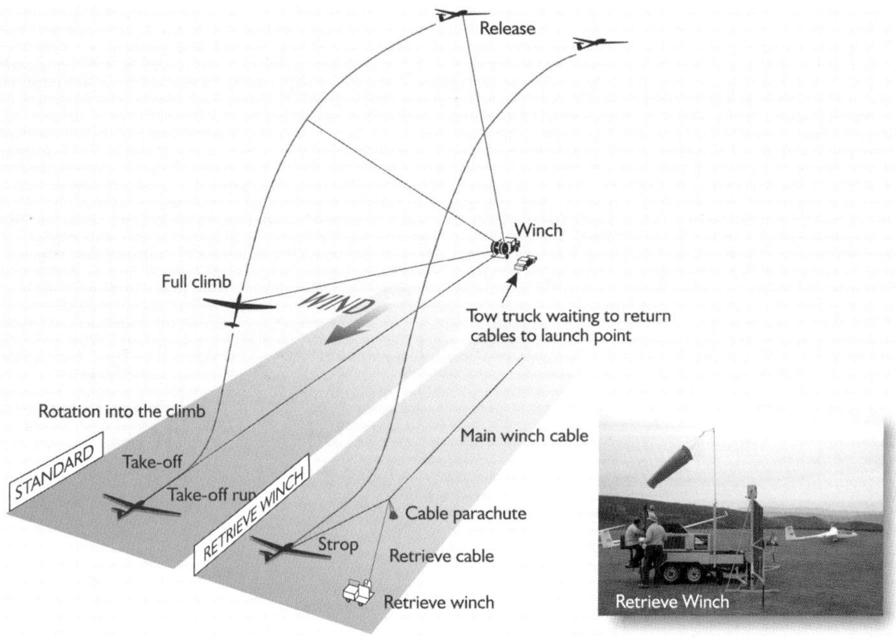

Release
Winch
Full climb
WIND
Tow truck waiting to return cables to launch point
Rotation into the climb
Main winch cable
STANDARD
Take-off
Take-off ru
RETRIEVE WINCH
Cable parachute
Strop
Retrieve cable
Retrieve winch
Retrieve Winch

The winch launch sequence.

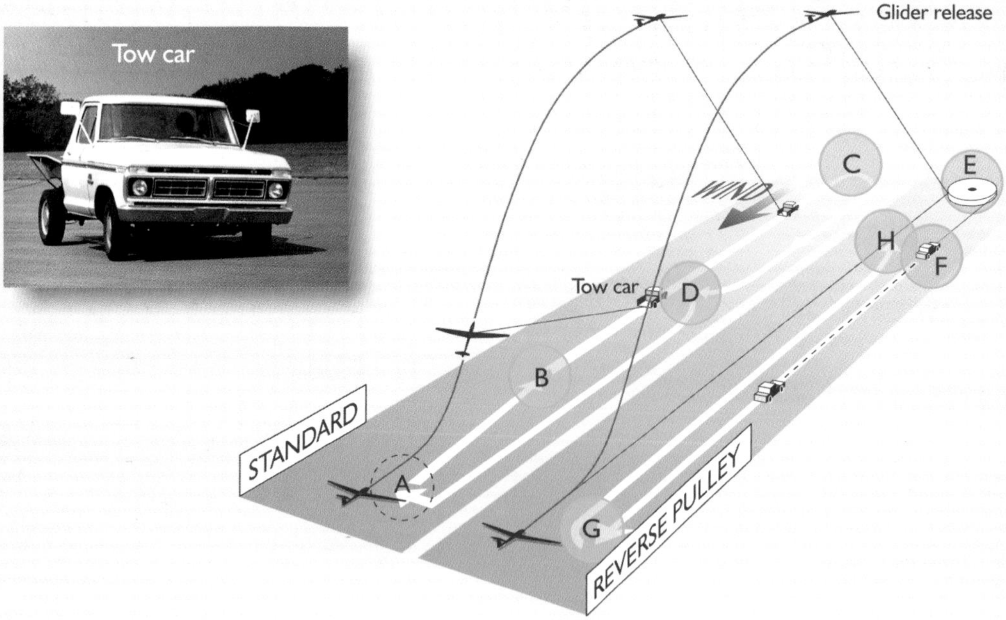

Tow car
Glider release
C
E
WIND
H
F
Tow car
D
B
STANDARD
A
G
REVERSE PULLEY

The auto-tow launch sequence.

condition and long enough to make auto-towing an effective means of launching.

The weak link/parachute set-up is either the same as or very similar to the one used for winching. Most auto-tows use a single solid cable of fixed length, whereas most winches use stranded wire cable which effectively gets shorter during a launch.

The two basic types of auto-tow, referred to in the diagram opposite, are the 'standard' and the 'reverse pulley' methods.

The standard method is straightforward. A length of cable is laid out from A to B, with the tow car attached to one end and the glider to the other. At the appropriate signal the tow car accelerates away and tows the glider into the air. Some way down the runway, but not at the end, the glider will reach the top of the launch and release the cable. The tow car continues on until the cable parachute has dropped to the ground, releases its end of the cable at

C, drives back to D to pick up the glider end and return it to the launch point. The tow car then returns to B, hooks on, and begins the process again.

The reverse pulley is an alternative. The cable runs from the launch point around a large pulley (E) at the upwind end of the runway. The tow car hooks on at the pulley end at F, the glider at the other. After the appropriate signals the tow car launches the glider as normal. The reverse pulley has two advantages:

1) The tow truck driver can see the glider during the most critical part of the launch without having to look back over his shoulder or use a mirror
2) The cable can be the length of the run, which can lead to slightly higher launches

The drawback is the pulley, which has to have a fairly large diameter and needs to be mounted either on a heavy truck

Winch launch. Taking up slack.

Aerotowing.

of its own, or fixed in the ground. With either method the piano wire that is normally used wears quite quickly on the runway's hard surface, but it is cheaper than the stranded wire normally used for winching.

AEROTOWING

Aerotowing involves launching the glider behind a suitable tow-plane, (see figure below) and has some advantages over the other launch methods. The operation requires less space overall, needs fewer people and the gliders don't have to release in exactly the same place every time. As against that, aerotow launches can be expensive and the launch rate, given an average turnround time of about ten minutes, tends to be slower, though not always so. During major competitions ten or more tow-planes can be operating continuously to launch as many as sixty gliders into the air within the hour stipulated by the competition rules. The sight is impressive, full of bustle and activity. In short bursts the launch rate can be one every 30 secs. This can't be achieved with winching because the launch itself takes some time, and while it is going on it isn't usually safe to launch anything else unless the take-off strip is sufficiently wide to allow a simultaneous aerotow (unlikely), or the take-off runs diverge markedly.

CATAPULT/BUNGY LAUNCHING (PRONOUNCED BUN-JEE)

A handful of clubs occasionally still use this method of launching, but small groups have been known to sneak off to mountainous areas and catapult themselves into the blue. Auto-bungy systems using a minimal crew have

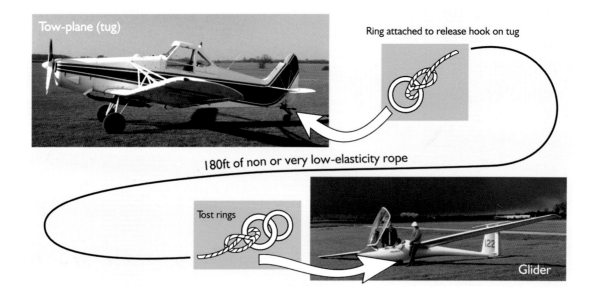

Aerotow launch set-up.

been known, but bungying normally requires at least seven fairly fit and willing volunteers to make it work. You also need to start from the top of a suitably shaped hill. If the brow is sharp and cliff-like, then turbulence in the lee becomes a problem, and the bungy crew just fall over the edge! The ideal hill has a smooth brow and a smooth slope leading up to it.

Bungying requires a brisk to strong wind blowing straight onto and up the face of the hill. This provides a band of rising air, which can extend a long way in front of and above the forward edge of the hill. The bungy is laid out in a 'vee' in front of the launch point, which may be little more than a small concrete chock set in the ground on

the brow of the hill, or a temporary hole dug with someone's heel. The pilot(s) strap themselves into the glider well back from the edge of the hill, out of the strongest wind, and the glider is then towed to the chock and either held there by the pilot using the wheel brake, or by somebody at the back hanging onto the tail. If the glider has a nose skid, the tail may be held very high to jam the skid onto the ground as a brake.

The 'vee' end of the bungy is hooked onto the glider's winch hook via a Tost ring and a short length of rope. The bungy crew, usually three or four to a side, take up their positions at the free ends of the 'vee'. At the signal 'RUN!' from the wingtip holder they race off

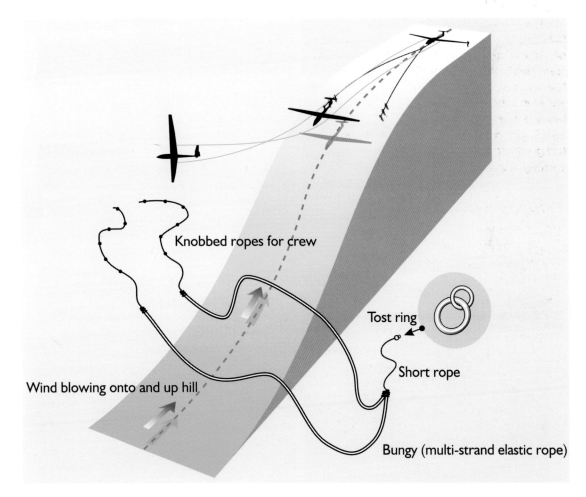

Knobbed ropes for crew

Tost ring

Short rope

Wind blowing onto and up hill

Bungy (multi-strand elastic rope)

Bungy launch set-up.

1 - Strong wind blowing straight onto hill

2 - Unpack the hangar

3 - Lay out and check the bungy

4 - Pilots strap into glider in lee of hangar

5 - Glider towed out to bungy point

6 - Bungy crew prepare to ...

7 - ...take up slack and wait for all-out signal

8 - At signal, they run until the bungee is fully stretched

9 - Wingman and tail holder release glider

10 - Pilot releases bungy, and flies the glider ....

11 - ... a short way out from the hill before turning left or right

down the hill and stretch the bungy as far as they can. The pilot then releases the wheel brake, or the tail holder lets go, and the glider rolls forward out of the chock, taking off within a few yards after a very smooth and gentle acceleration.

The pilot keeps the glider fairly close to the slope of the hill initially, in order to accelerate further, and releases the bungy when it is slack – if he does anything else the bungy crew will dramatically go head over heels. The glider flies out away from the hill, then turns to track along it, climbing in the rising air. The bungy crew then gather themselves and the rope and hike back up to the top in order to fling off the next glider.

The team effort involved is considerable, which is, sadly, one reason why bungy launching is now so rare. Bungy ropes are expensive and need to be in tip-top condition to avoid what might be termed misfires. Nevertheless, if you ever get the chance to try a bungy launch (not the far more hair-raising bungy jump), then do – it is a magical way of taking to the air. The Midland Gliding Club on the Long Mynd, Shropshire, still bungy occasionally.

OPPOSITE: *Bungying at the Long Mynd.*

5 What's in the Cockpit?

LOCATION OF THE CONTROLS

The major controls and what they do has already been described. Their disposition in the cockpit is standard, and more or less as illustrated opposite.

Some, but not all of the knobs and levers in the cockpit are colour coded according to an international standard:

Yellow   The yellow knob is used to attach and release the launch cable

Red   There are often several red levers in the cockpit which are either canopy locks and/or canopy jettison levers. Check with your instructor which does what before using any of them

Blue   The airbrakes control the rate of descent of the glider

Green   The trimmer is an aid to stress-free flight

Use of all the above is described in more detail later. Even if the glider has a retractable undercarriage – and most training two-seaters do not – or a flap operating lever (training two-seaters don't usually have flaps either), they won't be colour coded. So don't pull any levers or knobs until you know what they're connected to! Most gliders have wheel-brakes, which will be operated in one of three ways:

1) By a separate bicycle brake type lever on the stick. But beware, on some gliders the trim lever is on the stick (see Chapter 9 for trim)

2) By a separate lever or knob which is usually on the cockpit wall to your left (cockpits are laid out for right-handed people)

3) Linked to the airbrakes. When these are fully deployed, the last inch or so of airbrake lever travel will operate the wheel-brake

The wheel-brake is there to be used, but don't rely on it totally. If the ground is damp or wet some types of wheel-brake don't work at all, and with the others it is very easy to lock the wheel (no ABS here) and continue to skid merrily onwards. In all cases avoid harsh application of the wheel-brake during the landing run, particularly if the ground is soft: at best you'll gouge out a huge groove, at worst you'll get that and have the glider swivel round and go sideways or backwards, which may not do it much good.

In some single-seaters the wheel-brake is operated by pushing on both rudder pedals.

Other knobs and levers are likely to be an adjuster to allow you to move the rudder pedals to a comfortable position, and various ventilator knobs which can occasionally be confused with something else (for example, the canopy release), so watch out for that. If the glider is equipped to carry water ballast there will be a lever to pull to jettison the water.

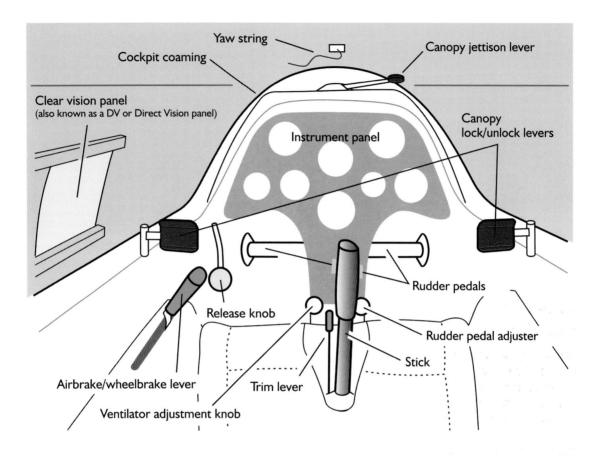

Cockpit – the controls.

INSTRUMENTATION

The position of individual instruments in the typical panel illustrated overleaf is not standardized, so the first thing you should do when you look at any panel is locate the air speed indicator. Ideally it should be at the top of the panel, though not necessarily in the centre. There ought to be a standard layout, but there isn't, largely because panels vary in shape, as do pilots and the size of some of the instruments. The depth of the space behind the panel may be the deciding factor in instrument location; some require more than others.

PITOT AND STATIC

Most of the instruments in a glider work by measuring pressure differences of one sort or another, and do this via two ports or openings in the glider, called the pitot

(pronounced pee-toe) and static. The pitot, usually a 'pot pitot', is set into the nose of the glider. The pot is like a small can with one end chopped off, and is open directly forward into the airflow (see diagram overleaf). The pitot tube itself passes through the pot, as illustrated, and contains a small hole which faces backwards, chiefly to prevent it becoming blocked by rain or dust and dirt. The static ports are usually paired and located somewhere on each side of the fuselage in a place where local variations in pressure are as small as possible. The static tubes are flush to the surface and open at right angles to the airflow. Their chief purpose is to 'sample' the ambient or local atmospheric pressure.

Both the altimeter and the airspeed indicator use the static as a reference point, rather like the zero on a rule, whereas the variometer uses the static more as a vent. The illustration on page 49 indicates where the static (S) and

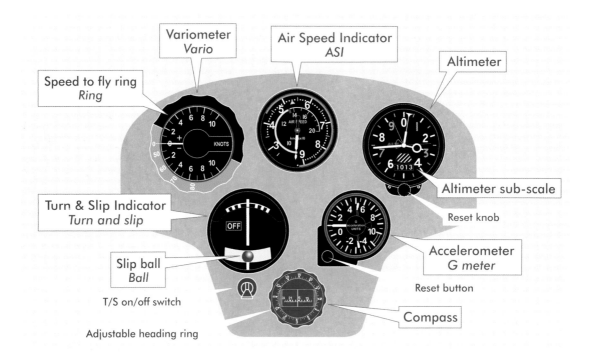

Speed to fly ring
Ring

Variometer
Vario

Air Speed Indicator
ASI

Altimeter

Turn & Slip Indicator
Turn and slip

Slip ball
Ball

T/S on/off switch

Adjustable heading ring

Altimeter sub-scale

Reset knob

Accelerometer
G meter

Reset button

Compass

Cockpit – the instruments.

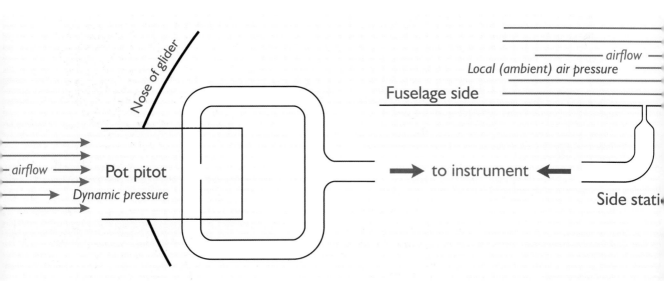

Nose of glider

airflow

Local (ambient) air pressure

Fuselage side

airflow

Pot pitot

Dynamic pressure

to instrument

Side static

Pitot and static.

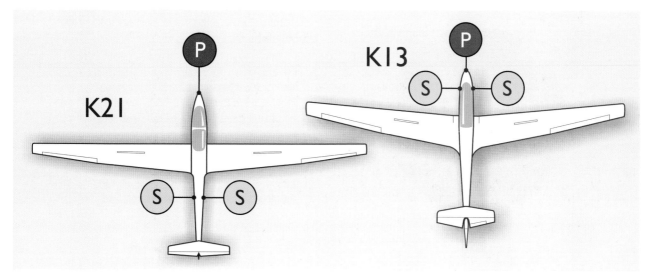

Location of pitot and static.

the pitot (P) ports are located for a K21 and a K13, two common two-seaters. How some of the instruments make use of these two ports is described below.

AIR SPEED INDICATOR (ASI)

The ASI (pronounced 'Ay Ess Eye') indicates airspeed but, surprisingly, not by direct measurement of the airflow/glider velocity. Instead, it measures a dynamic pressure identical to the one you feel when the wind blows against you. A flexible internal capsule in the ASI is open to the pitot, and the surrounding instrument case is connected to the static ports. As the glider moves along air is pushed into the capsule. Since the entry is also the exit, the faster the glider flies the more air goes in and then can't get out again, so the capsule's internal pressure rises and it expands. The opposite happens when the glider slows down.

The expansions and contractions of the capsule are magnified by a suitable mechanism and translated to a pointer on a circular scale. In the UK this is normally marked in knots (nautical miles per hour, or kt for short). Conveniently, 1kt is almost exactly 100ft/min.

Before take-off always make a mental note of where the zero is on the ASI; instruments differ. The best and most common position is with the zero at the bottom of the dial, as shown. For most normal speeds this puts the needle in

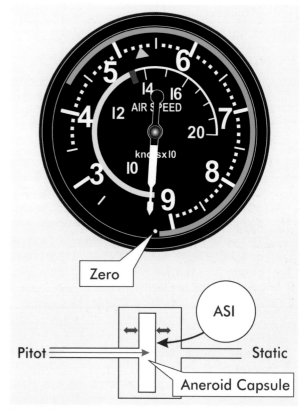

Air speed indicator.

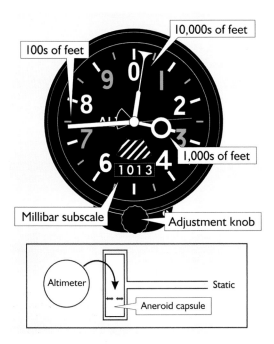

100s of feet

10,000s of feet

1,000s of feet

Millibar subscale

Adjustment knob

Altimeter

Static

Aneroid capsule

Altimeter.

the upper half of the instrument, nearer to the top of the panel where it is easy to see out of the corner of your eye – particularly useful during the launch, approach and landing.

ALTIMETER

The altimeter indicates altitude and is basically a barometer. The instrument is not connected to the pitot, but either to the static vents or left open to the cockpit. Inside the altimeter's casing there is a sealed (aneroid) capsule to which the dials/needles are attached by an appropriate mechanism. As the glider climbs, the pressure in the case (ie the outside air pressure at the static ports) drops and the air in the sealed capsule expands, moving the pointers to read a gain of altitude. When the glider descends the reverse happens.

There are typically three needles on most altimeters. One – usually with a ring on it – indicates hundreds of feet, another indicates thousands, and the third and sometimes shortest needle, tens of thousands of feet. The inset subscale gives you the barometric pressure, usually in millibars (mb), at the altitude to which the altimeter has been zeroed. The altimeter illustrated has a subscale setting of 1013mb, and reads 2,740ft.

There are two important things you need to know about pressure altimeters:

1) The mechanism will often stick, but temporary as this may be, when you're starting to look a bit low, don't rely on what the altimeter says. Below about 1,000ft from the ground, judging height by eye gets more and more accurate, the altimeter less so

2) An indicated 4,000ft on the altimeter won't necessarily put you level with the crest of a 4,000ft high mountain. The mountain's height is measured from mean sea level, and is fixed; the altimeter, on the other hand, translates into feet (in the UK) the difference in pressure between where it was zeroed and where it is now: in other words, its accuracy in terms of real height depends crucially on what you set the subscale to initially.

For example, almost all training flights are local, and whatever the height of the home airfield above sea level, the altimeter will always be set to zero (0ft) before take-off. If you then land somewhere else it is highly unlikely that the altimeter will read zero when you touch down. The instrument is also unable to distinguish between changes in pressure caused by the glider climbing or descending and those caused by the weather, such as approaching meteorological highs or lows.

THE ALTIMETER AND FLIGHT LEVELS

Strictly speaking, the only times in gliding when you need to rely on an altimeter are (1) to tell you when to go on oxygen (usually about 10,000ft above sea level), (2) to help you work out whether you're high enough to make it back to base or not, and more crucially, (3) to keep you out of restricted airspace – of which there is rather a lot in the UK, and not all of it starting at sea level.

You'll need to be properly briefed on what you can and can't pass through in terms of airspace, but the airways that criss-cross the country are, amongst some other areas, completely forbidden territory to gliders. The upper and lower limits of airways are almost always defined in terms of flight levels, and these are based on what an altimeter reads when its subscale is set to 1013mb. The chief advantage of this internationally agreed setting is that

imeter related terms you will come across:
E = altimeter subscale setting needed for altimeter to read zero when you're on the ground
NH = subscale setting needed for altimeter to read your altitude above sea level
(whether you're on the ground or not)
NE = indicated altitude when subscale is set to 1013mb

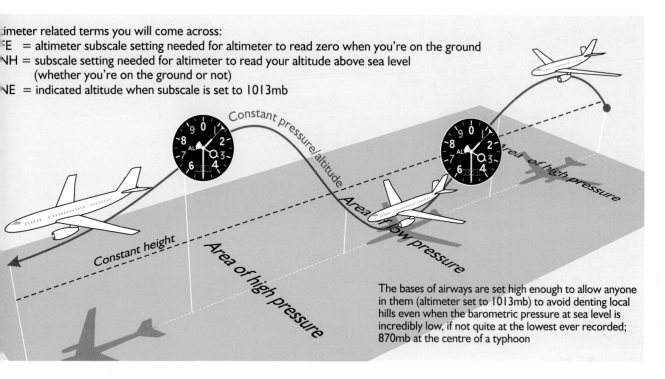

The bases of airways are set high enough to allow anyone in them (altimeter set to 1013mb) to avoid denting local hills even when the barometric pressure at sea level is incredibly low, if not quite at the lowest ever recorded; 870mb at the centre of a typhoon

The altimeter and flight levels.

everyone who uses it is effectively measuring from the same world-wide baseline, even if that – since it is driven by the weather – continually wanders up and down more or less at random (see above).

An airway might stretch from FL 50 to FL 210 (nominally from 5,000ft to 21,000ft), but because of pressure changes caused by the weather, or just by an aircraft travelling from one area to another, on one day FL50 would be 4,950ft above sea level, and on another 5,143ft. When glider pilots have to pass under airways they will set the altimeter subscale to 1013mb. Depending on the atmospheric pressure on the day, this reset can occasionally result in large apparent gains or losses in height. Pressure changes with height at about 1mb per 30ft (at sea level), so an altimeter set to a local pressure of 1024mb and reading 4,800ft, will read 5,130ft when reset to 1013mb. If the airway's base was FL50 the glider must descend by at least 130ft to avoid infringement. It is therefore best to avoid drama and possible prosecution by setting the altimeter to 1013mb some while before you actually arrive where you need to use it.

VARIOMETER

This is a vital piece of equipment for a glider, and if you wish to use any form of rising air to soar, is more important than the ASI or the altimeter. The variometer tells you how fast the glider is ascending or descending. It is a pressure instrument, like most of the others, but one that measures the flow of air caused by pressure differences between a specially insulated flask called the capacity, and the static ports.

When a glider flies into rising air and is carried upwards, the pressure of the surrounding atmosphere (the ambient or static pressure) falls. With the pressure in the capacity now higher than the static, air flows from the flask towards the static ports, passing through the variometer on its way and deflecting the instrument's pointer upwards, telling the pilot that the glider is climbing. Likewise, if the glider is descending, the static pressure will be higher than the capacity pressure, so the air flows in the opposite direction, deflecting the pointer downwards. You might think that the pilot would know whether the glider was

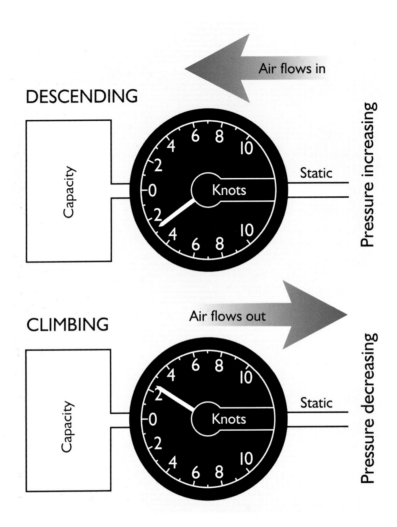

DESCENDING

Air flows in

Capacity

Knots

Static

Pressure increasing

CLIMBING

Air flows out

Capacity

Knots

Static

Pressure decreasing

Variometer.

going up or down anyway, but it is often difficult to tell, particularly if the rate is very slow and/or steady. The majority of electronic variometers don't measure flow, but calculate and display the rate of change of pressure at the static ports. Whilst they are extremely sensitive and could, in principle, display even the tiniest and most fleeting of pressure fluctuations, in practice they are designed to filter most of them out, to avoid completely baffling the pilot.

Most variometers are equipped with an adjustable MacCready or speed to fly ring marked with a set of speeds. This useful piece of equipment is discussed briefly in the chapter on cross country flying.

Variometer – audio unit

When trying to make best use of rising air it is all too easy to become mesmerized by the variometer readings and forget to look out. It is no exaggeration to say that this is exceptionally dangerous. To help glider pilots keep their heads 'out of the office', almost every glider with an electric variometer has a unit attached which gives audible indications of whether the glider is climbing or descending, and how fast. The noises vary according to variometer design, and confusingly, the noise for 'up' on one may be used to signal 'down' on another. There seems no agreed standard on this and the various squeaks and noises are, on the whole, typical 'cheap circuit electronics' and can grate after a bit. Luckily, audio units are usually equipped with volume controls.

COMPASS

Glider compasses are always magnetic compasses and require careful adjustment in situ on the ground (a process known as 'swinging the compass') before they will give accurate enough readings in the air. The standard binnacle or panel mounted compass tends to gyrate wildly if the glider is doing anything other than flying in a steady straight line, and after the completion of any manoeuvre will take a few seconds to settle down. The rotatable ring round the outside of the 'in-panel' compass illustrated allows you to set your course and easily work out reciprocal (back in the other direction) headings.

THE YAW STRING

This excellent and cheap piece of equipment is also one of the most useful. A thin piece of string or wool, about 4–5ins long, is attached along the canopy centreline and easily within your view. Ideally this string should always be pointing straight towards you, even during turns. Broadly speaking the glider was designed so that drag at any speed is always as low as possible when the airflow is approaching from directly ahead, in line with the fuselage. If the glider is slipping or skidding sideways the string will indicate inefficient flight (usually referred to as unbalanced flight) by blowing out to one side or the other. For example, if the string blows out to the right, then the airflow is coming from the left and you need some left rudder to swing the fuselage back in line with the airflow direction. Though both the string and the slip ball in the Turn and Slip (T/S) indicate whether you are in balanced flight or not, they do so in entirely different ways; one using the airflow direction, as described, and the other using the apparent direction of gravity. Slightly confusingly, the result is that if the string flies out to the right the ball will slide off to the left. The string is far more sensitive to slip and skid than the ball. How to get either/both back in the middle without making things worse is described under 'coordination' in Chapter 9.

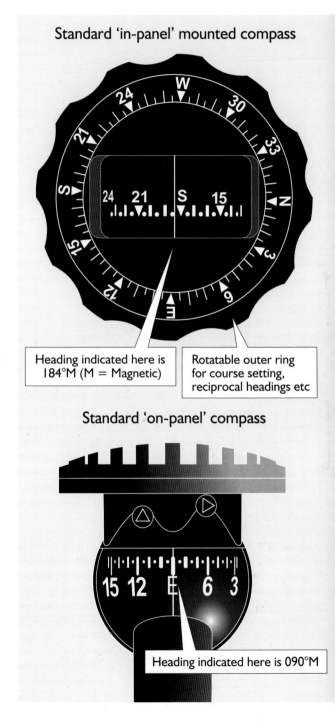

Standard 'in-panel' mounted compass

Heading indicated here is 184°M (M = Magnetic)

Rotatable outer ring for course setting, reciprocal headings etc

Standard 'on-panel' compass

Heading indicated here is 090°M

Two types of magnetic compass.

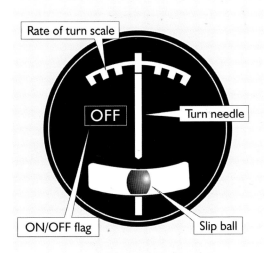

Turn and slip indicator.

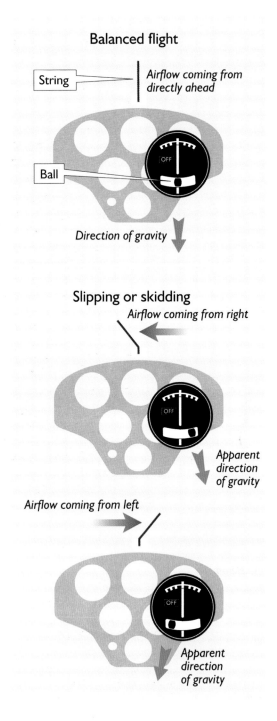

Ball and string.

TURN AND SLIP (T/S)

If there are no external visual cues – for example, you are in cloud and unable to see anything except the cockpit and perhaps as far out as the wingtips – it is impossible to maintain control of the aircraft for more than about 30 seconds without having some form of instrumentation to indicate what is happening. Without the appropriate clues the brain relies upon those which are provided by the apparent direction and strength of gravity, and unfortunately, changes in G can result in very strong sensations that X is happening when in fact the reality is Y, and this leads rapidly to complete disorientation. The pilot must rely exclusively on the instruments, and to maintain control needs two basic pieces of information: 1) the aircraft's pitch attitude (nose up or down), and 2) whether it is banked or not.

In free flight a glider's speed is closely related to its pitch attitude, so the ASI won't tell you if you are turning or not. The T/S will, but not by measuring bank directly. What it indicates is:

(a) how fast the nose is moving left or right along the horizon (the instrument is measuring yaw rather than bank), and

(b) whether the glider is in balanced flight or not (see

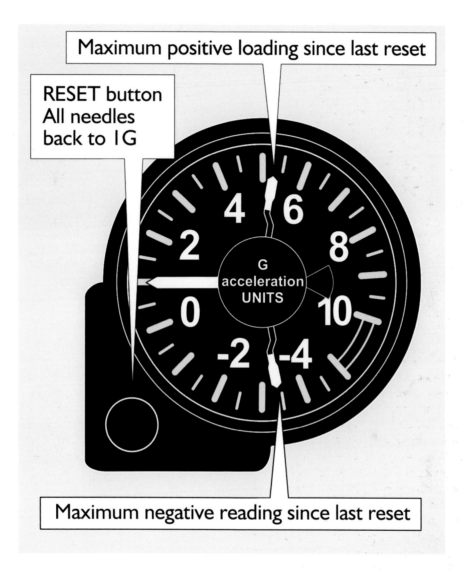

Maximum positive loading since last reset

RESET button
All needles
back to 1G

G
acceleration
UNITS

Maximum negative reading since last reset

Accelerometer.

notes below and the section on coordination in Chapter 9).

The turn needle is attached to an electrically driven gyroscope and will only work if the instrument is switched on. The ball, on the other hand, sits in a curved and liquid filled tube and works without batteries to tell you the apparent direction of gravity.

A glider may be equipped with an artificial horizon, which provides the pilot with a direct pictorial representation of nose attitude and angle of bank. Artificial horizons are rather powerful guzzlers of electrical juice, are often quite heavy, and if the attitudes become extreme they can 'topple'; neither of you then know which way is up.

SZD Junior cockpit and panel.

THE ACCELEROMETER OR G METER

We've already talked a little previously about loads and G, but it bears repeating that almost without exception any manoeuvre a glider makes will result in load/G changes. For example, when you bank a glider to turn, the steeper and faster the rate of turn the heavier the glider and you become.

In some circumstances you can temporarily become lighter, or even weigh nothing at all. The accelerometer measures these changes in G (the instrument is usually referred to as a G meter), but only in relation to the vertical loads on the glider, unless the instrument has been mounted skew.

There are structural limits to the loads a glider can withstand, but most gliders are a great deal stronger than the average airliner. In general, if you don't subject a glider to loads of more than +5G or −2G at a normal, working range of speeds (see later notes on the placard and speed limitations), you're not likely to break anything. There are several ifs and buts to that rather bald statement, one being that the G meter does not measure all the loads to which a glider is subjected. Every gliding club has someone technically adept enough who can explain the ins and outs of design limitations, manoeuvring envelopes and all the rest; go to them if you'd like to know more.

The G meter has three pointers, two of which indicate the maximum and minimum vertical G loadings to which the glider has been subjected since the instrument was last zeroed. The third tells you what's happening at this instant. The reset button is usually to the bottom left of the instrument, (see illustration), and you either push it in or turn it slightly to reset the needles. Notice that they reset at one, not zero!

GPS (GLOBAL POSITIONING SYSTEM)

Since the first edition the navigational picture has changed enormously. In gliding, at least, electronic navigation has taken over almost completely from paper maps, and a GPS unit is the navigational instrument of choice despite it having a number of drawbacks which make it less than 100 per cent reliable. One is that the entire system can be turned off in an instant by the people who look after it, and another is that it isn't difficult to jam. You'll know about the first if it happens, but not necessarily about the second. In any case, while these electronic navigational aids aren't currently standard pieces of equipment in all club gliders – single-seaters especially – they will become so. Chapter 12 goes into a bit more detail.

6 Gliding Basics

How quickly you learn to glide will depend on the amount of time you can put towards it, and your ability. It is exceedingly rare for people never to go solo, but for a very few the training process can become prolonged, either because the motor skills are lacking or for some other reason such as time or funds available. Age is no bar, but generally speaking, if you have no previous piloting experience, then the older you are the longer it will take for you to go solo. A sixteen-year-old might solo in 40 flights (the current lowest age limit for solo is 16), but someone of 60 might take three times as long.

Disability won't necessarily prevent you from learning to glide, but this will depend somewhat on the disability and, in some cases, on the availability of suitably adapted controls. Either way, you need to be reasonably healthy and to be able to see well. Wearing glasses is no bar. The medical requirements are less onerous than those required for power flying. Europe seems to have other views about that. The outcome is unsure, but the BGA and the Clubs will have more up-to-date information than this book can provide.

At present (January 2012) every gliding club will require you to sign a declaration (see example), countersigned by your doctor, to the effect that you are reasonably healthy and not suffering from any condition likely to incapacitate you. The current standards are based, simply, on those required for the UK driver's licence.

GENERAL FITNESS

Never drink alcohol before flying. To quote from the BGA Instructors' Manual:

> The uncoordinating effects of alcohol are indisputable, unless of course you happen to be drunk and argumentative with it … any residual alcohol in your system will have an adverse effect

Example medical declaration.

(on your reaction times) which may not be very apparent to anyone, least of all you...

The same goes for some medicines, and for most of the so-called recreational drugs which, legal or not, are just as bad for your general awareness and physical co-ordination as alcohol.

Don't fly if you're tired, or upset, or have just had a row with somebody. If you are preoccupied, whatever the reason, then you probably won't pay much attention to the flying. If you are solo you will be at far greater risk than you're likely to realize, and you will learn less if you are under tuition.

THE BASIC KIT
FOR THE AIRFIELD

Airfields can be some of the coldest and draughtiest places on earth, even when the weather seems quite warm. There can also be very little shade, on the ground or in the air. It is best to gather together a gliding club kit that will contain everything you might need at the airfield, for any weather.

If you normally wear a skirt, don't. Use slacks or trousers. You will need warm clothing, thick socks, good boots or walking shoes, a sun hat with a narrow brim (a wide one can interfere with your lookout in the air), sun cream with a very high UV rating, good sun glasses – preferably Polaroids or proper aviation sunglasses – and a large water bottle or something similar.

When it is hot and the sun is bright it is best to keep yourself reasonably well covered and wear long-sleeved shirts to avoid being burnt. The wind on warm days keeps you nicely cool by evaporating your sweat, but though this will make you feel comfortable, the life-giving water inside you is being quietly wafted away.

Unfortunately, due to a quirk of biology, you won't start to feel thirsty until you are already well dehydrated. If you get a headache, it is too late; no matter how much you drink now, you will only gradually re-hydrate and the headache will last a long time. Severe dehydration can cause complete incapacitation. On hot days, both on the ground and when airborne, it is best to drink smallish amounts of water often, and the hotter the day the more you'll need. Sugary drinks are sticky and messy when spilt, and tea and coffee are diuretics (small amount in now, large amount out a little later) so they can have the opposite effect to the one intended.

LOGBOOKS

The club will certainly provide you with a logbook. This will be the record of your flights, and a place where instructors make comments about the exercises you have done and what needs doing next. You will also be given a syllabus sheet and/or a progress record card of some description. The 'Serial number' of the flight is not the number of the flight as it appears on any log-sheet kept by the club, but a running total of all your flights. 'Date' is obvious as is the 'Glider type' (K13, K21, Puchacz etc) and the 'Place of launch'. The 'Type of launch' is usually filled in with just the initial letter – W for winch, A for aerotow, B for bungy, sometimes C (catapult) is used or M for auto-tow (motor). The 'Remarks' column is for comments from your

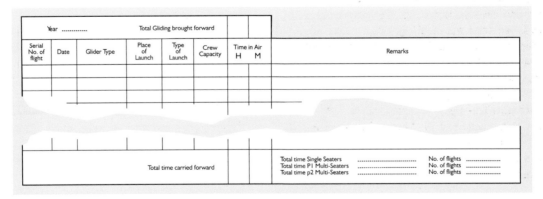

Logbook.

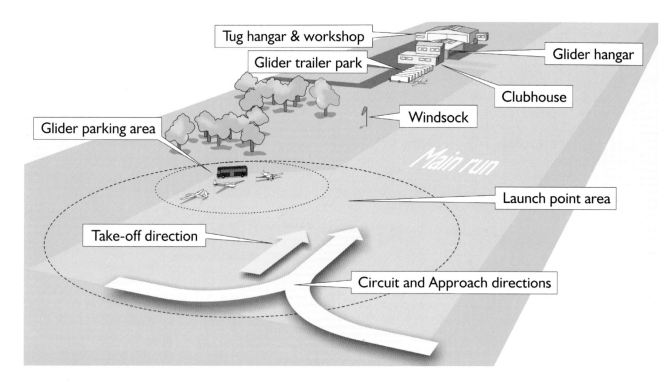

Tug hangar & workshop

Glider trailer park

Glider hangar

Clubhouse

Windsock

Glider parking area

Main run

Launch point area

Take-off direction

Circuit and Approach directions

Basic airfield layout.

instructor on your flight, ie 'Good flight, did all of launch. Co-ordination!' – the last comment would suggest more practice at using the aileron and rudder together. The entry may also include some hint as to what to do next. Once solo you can scribble your own comments, but until then your Crew Capacity will always be P2, the pilot under instruction, and your instructor will always be P1, the pilot in charge. Keep the logbook and/or progress sheet up to date, and at the end of any instructional flight ask the instructor to fill in the Remarks section. He or she will normally do this as a matter of course, but if the day is particularly busy, they may forget.

MOVING AROUND THE AIRFIELD

Most of the advice on moving around on the airfield consists of a series of straightforward do's and don'ts, such as:

- Always have a good look around before crossing any open part of the gliding field – someone might be about to land there. Look downwind first, as this is where gliders are most likely to come from. Check all around the airfield for airborne gliders preparing to land (see circuit diagram in Chapter 9) just in case someone is tip-toeing in from low down
- When crossing any active area keep a constant lookout. Be particularly careful if you are setting off to retrieve a glider that has just landed. It is easy to look at that rather than what may be creeping up behind you
- Never walk in front of gliders waiting to launch, just in case they do
- Don't walk across cables and keep clear of winch/auto-tow parachutes and strops or ropes so that you aren't accidentally launched without a glider
- Keep clear of the tug aircraft's propeller. If you do need to approach the tug to talk to the pilot, do so from behind the wing, never in front

GROUND HANDLING

Moving gliders around on the ground

Though training gliders are, in fact, very strong, there are some areas and edges that you should avoid pushing against or using for lifting. These no-go areas depend sometimes on the material out of which the glider is made, but the general principles are:

- Definitely NO pushing on any of the moveable control surfaces (i.e. rudder, aileron, elevator, flaps)
- Don't push on anything that gives
- Don't push or lift anywhere on the tailplane – if the glider is equipped with handles or handling bars on the rear fuselage, use these
- Never move the glider by pulling or pushing on the canopy, which is easy to damage and expensive to repair
- Don't push on the trailing edges of the wings of wood and fabric gliders except right up against the fuselage
- To avoid extra stresses and strains on the structure, always make sure that the tail-skid/wheel and nose-skid/wheel are both off the ground before you swing the glider round

Towing a glider out to the launch point or back to the hangar

The normal method of moving a glider around at the launch point is for two or more people to push or pull by hand. For longer distances, where pushing would be the healthiest but maybe not the preferred option, a car is used with either tow-out gear or a small crew. A tow-out kit consists of a wing dolly, a tail dolly, a bar to hitch the glider to a car, and requires only the car driver. If you use a tow rope you will need someone on the wingtip, someone near the nose to prevent the glider running into the back of the tow vehicle and possibly someone near the tail to help the glider round corners without the tail or nose-skid/wheel dragging on the ground.

When towing out using a rope, don't drive too fast – everybody just falls over! Likewise, if there is any appreciable wind from the nose, the increased airflow over the wings can cause the glider to take-off, and the windier the day or the faster the tow-out the more likely this is to

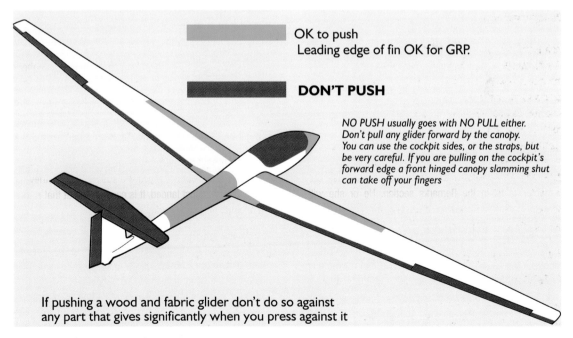

OK to push
Leading edge of fin OK for GRP.

DON'T PUSH

NO PUSH usually goes with NO PULL either. Don't pull any glider forward by the canopy. You can use the cockpit sides, or the straps, but be very careful. If you are pulling on the cockpit's forward edge a front hinged canopy slamming shut can take off your fingers

If pushing a wood and fabric glider don't do so against any part that gives significantly when you press against it

Where and where not to push.

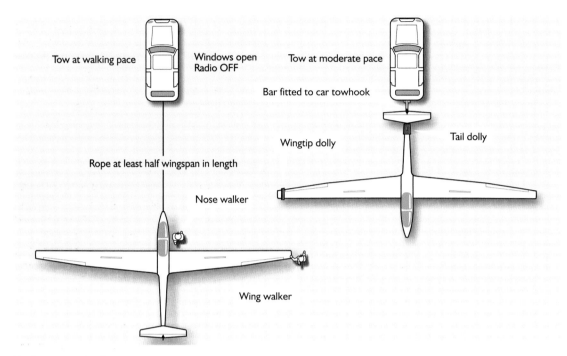

Towing out methods.

happen. Four or more people might be needed for a tow-out, depending on the wind strength and the type of glider. In a strong wind the walker(s) on the nose may need to hold the nose down, or one of them to be strapped into the glider's front seat to add weight and produce the same effect. Just in case the glider should take-off it is best if whoever is strapped in can actually fly it.

The rope ought to be at least as long as half the glider's wingspan so that if the car stops suddenly, or the glider starts to over-run, the wingtip holder can hold back and the glider will swing round and miss the car. The car driver should keep one or both side windows open and the radio/music player off, other than a radio used for winch launch point communication, so that he or she can hear any instructions shouted by the crew, such as STOP!

When using tow-out gear resist the easy temptation to go fast – the glider can start bouncing up and down quite violently and get damaged. Remember, too, that without a wingtip holder you may not be very good at judging exactly where the wingtip is, and with the glider being towed backwards the wing's trailing edge, which is quite sharp, will be acting like a scythe, so be careful.

Parking gliders

It is important to park gliders correctly when they aren't being used because the wind can otherwise blow them over onto their backs or move them around. The general rule is that gliders should be parked with the wind blowing at a shallow angle over the trailing edges of the wings so that they produce little or no lift. You can park the glider with the into-wind wing either down or up, and which wing you put on the ground depends largely on the glider. If the glider is very light (wooden gliders are particularly vulnerable) then always put the into-wind wing down and hold it there with the tyres that are usually scattered around gliding sites for this purpose.

Stick additional tyres under the nose and around the tail skid to prevent the glider weathercocking round to point into wind. Most modern gliders are heavier than wood and fabric gliders and can be parked with the into-wind wing up, unless the wind happens to be very strong. There is an awkward and not always easily remembered distinction between those gliders which must be parked with the into-wind wing down and those which can be parked with it up. This has arisen, in part, not because modern gliders don't

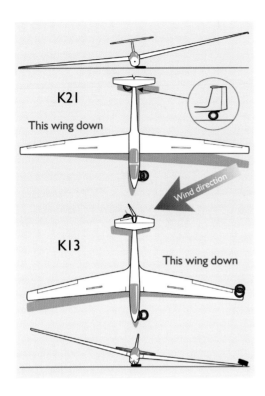

Parking gliders.

or can't blow over, but because they are rather easy to scratch! Tyres turn into scouring pads as airfield grit becomes embedded in them and UV light from the sun breaks their surfaces down into soot. Placing such objects on a pristine white wing can damage the finish and leave unsightly stains. If you are in any doubt as to the best parking method for a particular glider, ask your instructor.

OTHER GROUND JOBS

It is unlikely that you will be asked to do some of the jobs described below (e.g. launch co-ordinator) until you've been a member of the club for quite a while. As with many other items, there are variations in procedure between clubs and some of the separate jobs described may be rolled into one, but in all cases you will need a proper briefing beforehand.

Hooking on the cables

The glider end of any rope or cable has a set of interlinked Tost rings attached (see illustration below). The smaller of the two is the one that goes into the launch hook assembly. Many gliders have two launch hooks, one near the nose, for aerotowing, and

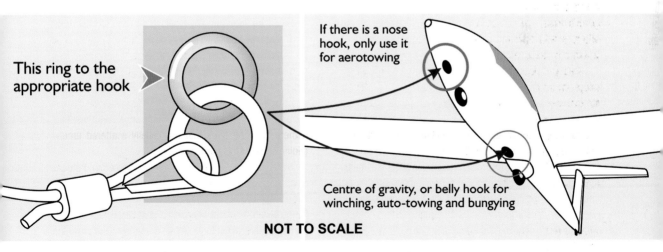

Tost rings and typical aerotow/winch hook positions.

Aerotow hook on the K21.

Tost weak link colour coding				
			Breaking load	
			DaN	lbs
Black	1		1000	2200
Brown	2		850	1870
Red	3		750	1650
Blue	4		600	1320
White	5		500	1100

Tost weak link ratings.

another near the glider's centre of gravity (the CG or belly hook), for every other type of launch. Some gliders have a belly hook only, but if the glider also has a nose hook, use that for aerotow in preference to the belly hook. Likewise, don't use a nose hook for winch or bungy launching. Winching on a nose hook usually results in a very low launch.

The photograph above illustrates the position of the aerotow hook on a K21, just ahead of the nosewheel. Note the ring that forms part of the release and into which the smaller of the Tost rings is inserted. The belly hook looks exactly the same, but is further back and more difficult to get at.

Weak links

Each glider has been designed to winch using a weak link of a specific strength. The links are colour coded according to their breaking load, as in the table above, and it is important to use the correct one. If the link is too weak it will break unnecessarily on the launch – they break sometimes anyway, but there's no point in making sure of it. If the link is too strong the glider can be subjected to loads for which it was not designed.

On the fuselage, next to the belly hook, there may be marked a coloured triangle indicating which link to use, but if

not, ask the pilot. Aerotow rope weak links, if used at all, usually consist of a short length of thinner rope at the tow plane end.

Hooking gliders on to the launch cable can be a muddy experience, as you will discover. When the pilot has completed the cockpit checks, he or she will say 'Hook on', pull on the cable release knob (usually known as the 'release'), and then say 'Open'. Take the smaller ring, push it vertically up into the ring that forms part of the hook assembly, and say 'Close'. The pilot will reply 'Close', and let go of the release knob. The release's internal hook will then pick up the smaller ring. Stand up and pull on the strop or the rope between the parachute and the weak link (see winch set-up diagram, Chapter 4) to check that the hook is secure. If it is you would normally say something theatrical to the pilot like 'You're on', or 'On and secure', and then get out of the way so that the launch can proceed.

Acting as a wingtip holder

Regardless of how many wheels a glider may have, they all sit, bicycle-like, along the fuselage centre line, and when the glider is at rest or moving along the ground too slowly for the controls to work, one wing will be on the ground. The wingtip holder's job is to keep the wings level during the initial stages of the take-off run. The glider will normally be hooked to the downwind cable of a pair first, but station yourself on the wingtip furthest away from any other cables that may be out. This also makes good sense in crosswinds because if you're on the other side the natural tendency of the glider to turn into wind will be towards you and you won't be in the best position to help prevent this – not unless you can run like a gazelle. Never put your fingers or hand into any wingtip holes or through any handling brackets. If the glider accelerates away abruptly you could be dragged away with it, or find yourself missing a finger or two.

It is up to the pilot to check whether the ground area ahead is clear of obstacles and the airspace above and ahead of the launch point clear of other aircraft. But the view directly backwards from most gliders is non-existent and the pilot has to rely on someone else, usually the wingtip holder, to check whether it is 'all clear, above and behind'. Are there tugs or gliders on the approach, or anyone approaching from odd directions who might have to land ahead of the glider about to launch? Are any airborne gliders or wandering powered aircraft going to conflict with the launch itself?

The launch signalling will usually be done by someone other than the wingtip holder. When the glider starts to roll don't hold back or push forward on the wingtip, just hold it lightly to provide support and run with the glider until the wingtip leaves your hand. When the wind is strong and straight down the take-off run you may only need to take a few steps, if that, before letting go.

Where cables are towed out in pairs (sometimes more), they can occasionally become crossed somewhere down the field. The cable being used for the launch, known as the live cable, can take the other cable(s) with it, either immediately the slack starts to be taken up – usually very obvious – or shortly after the glider has started rolling. This latter case is dangerous because the ostensibly free cable can go from zero to the speed of the active cable, which could easily be 50mph, in a split second. For those reasons never pick up or walk over a free cable when a glider is being launched on another.

Driving a cable retrieve truck

You won't be asked to tow out the cables from the winch to the launch point until you have been gliding for a while, but then make sure you are shown how to do it. If the job is done incorrectly, launching can be brought to a standstill, occasionally for hours, while the resulting cable tangles are sorted out.

Normally the launch cables need to be towed out in a straight line from the winch to the launch point to prevent them crossing over, and the tow must start and stop smoothly. Don't start to pull out a cable until instructed to by the winch driver as he or she may have a hand in one of the cable drums.

Keeping the flying list

On arriving at the airfield it is usual for pilots to put their name immediately on the flying list. This helps to sort out launch priority if there are any arguments over whose turn it is to fly next. Looking after the flying list is usually incorporated with some other launch point job.

Keeping the flying log

This is a straightforward book-keeping job which can become hectic at a busy club. The details needed for each log entry will depend on the club, but at the least will include the type of glider and/or the numbers or letters on the fin, the name of the pilot(s) and who was P1 or P2, the time of take-off (and landing), and the type of launch. If you are given this job, write neatly so that the keeper of the club statistics can tell the truth, and the treasurer can figure out whether the club is trading effectively or not.

Acting as a launch signaller/launch marshal

This is an important job. With the exception of bungying and aerotowing, the distance between the glider and the launch vehicle can be anything up to a mile. Signalling over these distances is provided either by lights, large dayglo covered bats or radio on a specially allocated frequency. After the glider has been hooked on and it is 'all clear, above and behind', the first part of any launch is to 'take up (the) slack' and remove any coils or bows in the rope or cable. Just before the cable tightens the 'all out' signal is given and the glider then accelerates away for take-off.

It is important that the signals be distinct, however they are given. For example, when giving 'take up slack' using a radio you would make a longish pause between each 'take up slack', whereas 'all out' would be repeated immediately and spoken slightly quicker. Giving 'take up slack' using lights would need a slowish background count with the

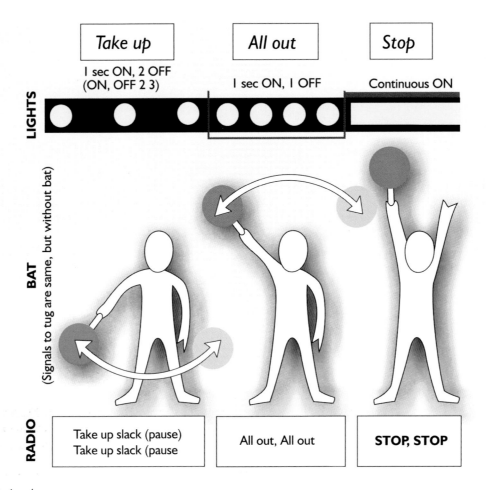

	Take up	All out	Stop
LIGHTS	I sec ON, 2 OFF (ON, OFF 2 3)	I sec ON, I OFF	Continuous ON
BAT (Signals to tug are same, but without bat)			
RADIO	Take up slack (pause) Take up slack (pause	All out, All out	**STOP, STOP**

Launch signals.

light on for about one second and then off for two seconds. 'All out' would be on for one second, off for one second. 'Stop' would be a continuous light. Note that if light signals are given too fast the lamp bulb filament may never stop glowing, and will look like a stop signal.

For aerotowing the signals are normally by hand, are often given by the wingtip holder (procedures differ between clubs) and are the same as those illustrated using the 'bat', but without the bat. A forward signaller may be needed opposite the tug to relay the signals from the launch controller to the tug pilot. If you are acting as a forward signaller don't stand too close to the line of take-off unless you want to get mown down – not only is the glider's span much larger than the tug's but it may not go quite straight to start with. When there's a crosswind, stand on the down-wind side of the glider and tug combination if possible.

The other part of a job which often falls into the 'herding cats' category may entail organizing the launch queue so that when the cables arrive there is someone ready to be launched immediately. This is important, because launch point delays can slow everything to a crawl. It's easy to regard this as acceptable if you're next to be launched, perhaps, but if you're a bit further down the queue you'll find that it isn't!

Winch driver/tow-car driver/tug pilot

You won't normally be asked to be a winch driver until you have graduated to flying on your own or 'gone solo'. Clubs prefer that anyone who drives/flies a launch vehicle is a glider pilot, but this is not essential and clubs do use excellent professional winch drivers who may never have

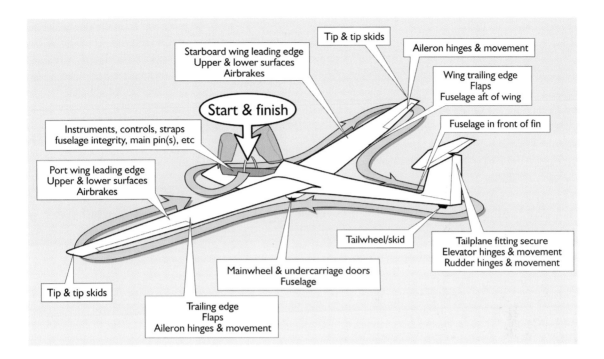

Daily Inspection (DI) sequence.

flown a glider. It is particularly important that tug pilots know where lift is likely to be and take gliders to it by the most direct route possible. The club will train you as a winch or auto-tow truck driver when the time comes. If you have a burning desire to be a tug pilot, talk to the club's Chief Tug Pilot about the requirements.

MISCELLANEOUS

Daily Inspections

While it is obligatory to do a DI (daily inspection) on a glider at the start of each flying day, you won't be allowed to do one until you have at least gone solo, and then only after several guided tours given by club instructors, or whoever the club has decided is responsible enough to teach you. Apart from the legal requirements relating to who is allowed to do what, you will as a matter of practicality need to know quite a lot about how gliders are built and work.

You begin and end at the cockpit. Whether you work your way round the glider clockwise or anti-clockwise doesn't matter much, providing you keep going the same way

throughout. Keep to the sequence, don't skip bits, and if you are interrupted go back at least one step before you continue. Similarly, unless you have a very good reason for doing so, don't interrupt anyone who is doing a DI.

Once you've done a DI you must sign the DI book – which you will find in the cockpit – to say whether the glider is airworthy or not. If it isn't, state exactly why. The DI book contains a record of all previous DIs, and, obviously, notes about any faults, major or minor. It is best not to read this before you start a DI. Having a fault pointed out makes it easier to find, of course, but may distract you from finding something less well signposted.

Undertaking a DI is a big responsibility because it is safety critical. If there is any doubt whatsoever in your mind about anything you come across, ask an instructor or someone with suitable experience for a second, perhaps even a third opinion. In aviation never assume that something is 'probably OK'. If anything goes wrong with your car you can usually pull in to the side of the road and study the problem at your leisure; with an aeroplane you almost always have to reach the ground first.

If the glider is not airworthy, sign the DI book to that effect and leave a note on one of the seats.

7 The Instruction

The whole purpose of your instruction is not just to teach you how to fly, but also how to look after yourself in the air. Flying is not particularly dangerous, but ignorance can put you at risk and inattention most certainly does. What your instructors are trying to do, in their several ways, is give you the tools, tell you how they work and show you how to use them correctly. Once satisfied that you can do everything reasonably well (you don't have to be perfect), they send you off on your own.

There is some slight variation between clubs, not in what they teach – that's standard – but the exact order in which they do things. Flying training begins by teaching you how to avoid damaging yourself or anything else on the airfield and on the ground, and then goes on to teach you the basic flying (handling) skills. You will be given a logbook and usually a syllabus card or progress sheet. There will be a list of items that must be covered, and your instructors will take you through all of them, step by step, signing them off as completed when you have reached an acceptable standard.

You may not always be signed off for exercises in the sequence outlined by the syllabus. Some exercises are very weather and cloudbase dependent. You won't be practising spins if the cloudbase is 1,000ft, total overcast. It is perfectly possible in most training gliders to spin deliberately at 900ft, do one complete turn and recover safely, if

low, but the margin for error here is far too small, so, sensibly, spin training takes place very much higher up. When the cloudbase is low you will concentrate on less height-sensitive exercises.

What you will find also is that some of the exercises appear to be in the wrong order. Flight begins with a take-off, but the training sequence – for very sound practical reasons – will turn it all about face. For example, you will begin learning to winch by flying the top of the launch and the release first, and the ground-run and take-off will be tackled last. As far as this book is concerned most, but not all, of the exercises described in Chapter 9 will be in the order encountered in flight. In other words, take-off will precede release.

Instructors will try to avoid introducing you to something new before they think you are ready for it. If you are having difficulty co-ordinating the controls you will find it almost impossible to fly in a straight line. If you cannot fly in a straight line there is no point in attempting the landing or the take-off, or having a go at the aerotow, because in all of these cases you will end up swooping majestically all over the place. You will feel that everything is out of control, and indeed, from your point of view, it is. That perception won't do wonders for your overall confidence, although be assured that your instructor will probably be relaxed, perhaps even entertained, by what is happening.

Canopies open on a K21.

PRE– AND POST–FLIGHT BRIEFINGS

Classroom and launch point briefings

Before each new exercise there will always be a briefing. This may take the form of a classroom briefing where you can ask questions and engage in leisurely debate without the immediate need to take-off and put everything to the test. If you are in any doubt about anything that you are told during a briefing, ask. The phrase 'Everybody clear on that?', even the somewhat rhetorical 'OK?!', often elicits no response, or 'Yes' as a default even when none of us is very clear about any of it. If we are part of a group it is easy, for all sorts of odd tribal reasons, to end up saying precisely the opposite of what we might if we were on our own. Regardless, if you don't understand anything, say so. The only silly question is 'Why are you asking questions?'

There will always be a much shorter pre-flight briefing at the launch point. Before your earliest flights you will probably be feeling a bit nervous anyway, so the shorter these briefings the better. They will consist largely of reminders of the purpose of the exercise to be carried out, a very brief description of what's going to happen, perhaps drawing your attention to some particular aspect of it, and what you're expected to do. Then you set off to do it. The instructor may give an airborne demonstration if necessary, but when you are doing the flying he or she will make appropriate comments or offer advice at the time which may just boil down to 'try X', or 'see what happens if you do Y', or will re-demonstrate. The process is repeated, in whole or part, throughout a number of flights until you reach a reasonable standard of proficiency. Practice is the key.

There will always be a de-briefing of some sort after the flight, a discussion of how well you did, and what you need to do next. In the early stages of your training, the de-brief will almost inevitably contain rather a lot of 'that's not the way to do it' – put less punchily, one hopes – but with plenty of encouragement for what you've done well. The majority of instructors can remember their own early difficulties in learning to fly, both psychological and otherwise, and will be as sympathetic to yours as they were aware of their own. If you do manage to do something really awful you'll be told what it was and how to avoid doing it the next time.

Though the emphasis will be on the practical handling skills necessary to fly a glider, there's much more to being a good pilot. You will need to lookout well. You also need to know and understand some of the theory, a large chunk of which has been covered already, and most of which is relatively straightforward. The biggest drawback of aerodynamic theory is that in most instances we literally can't see what it is that we are talking about. This makes the whole thing seem far more abstract and intractable than it really is, though in truth, some of it isn't completely straightforward – how wings work is one example of that. In any event, some knowledge of how gliders work is vital, and without it silly but understandable mistakes are easy to make.

An equally important part of gliding which the instruction aims at developing in you is judgement. It is pointless having good handling skills if you then, in effect, try and fly through a wall! We'll look briefly at judgement later even though it will be implicit in the descriptions of the various exercises.

An Important Form of Words

Over the course of many flights the training will result in a gradual transfer of control and responsibility from the instructor to you, the trainee. The instructor is always the P1 (pilot in command), even when the trainee (P2) is doing all the flying, but there should be no possibility of there being any doubt as to who is flying the glider at any given moment. To avoid two pilots fighting against each other, or nobody flying the glider at all (it has happened), the form of words used by the instructor when handing over control to you will be 'You have control'. You should put your hands and feet on the controls if they weren't there already, and reply 'I have control'. The instructor will then take his hands and feet off. Similarly, when he takes back control from you, he or she will say 'I have control'. You should then let go, get your hands and feet well clear of the controls, and reply 'You have control'.

There may be times when a polite and formal transfer of control is overtaken by events, so that 'I have control' becomes shortened to 'I have', or the instructor just takes control. The most likely but by no means inevitable time for this to happen is during your first few attempts at landing.

If you are told to 'follow through on the controls' when the instructor is demonstrating an exercise, hold the stick lightly, and rest your feet lightly on the rudder pedals. You need to be able to feel the controls moving without actually preventing them from doing so.

Time Considerations

Gliding can take up as much or as little of your time as you wish, but increasing numbers of us have less free time than we'd like, and cannot afford to spend much of it on an airfield. Many medium to large clubs run week-long courses, often residential, and if you're about to be overdrawn in time and patience, going on a course is a good way of learning how to glide. Courses have a continuity that weekend flying can sometimes lack, and you will very likely be with the same instructor throughout. As always in this country the weather is the big question mark.

However, even if your training is excellent and you have extraordinary aptitude, don't bet that you will go from knowing nothing at all about flying to solo in a week. The flight time to solo isn't as relevant as the number of launches, since these require landings as well. Launches to solo average between 50 and 60 for a winch, and rather less for aerotow. If the average flight time from a winch launch is, say, five minutes, that's just over four hours' flying time before you're on your own – rather less than seems to be necessary to learn to drive a car – but that four hours takes no account of how long you spend on the airfield. The number of aerotow launches to solo is lower, roughly 25 to 30, and the average flight time is about 15 minutes, at least five of which are spent on tow. You will get slightly more time airborne, but fewer landings and take-offs. Take your pick.

THE SYLLABUS

The BGA has an approved method of teaching, and a syllabus of subjects that must be covered. The syllabus will include the following items – Chapter 9 looks at some of them in more detail: Ground handling; Preparing for flight; Lookout and collision avoidance; Primary effects of the controls; Secondary or further effects of the controls; Use of the trimmer; Straight flight; Medium turns; Steep (or tight) turns; Straight stall; Effects of misuse of rudder; Accelerated or high speed stalls; Stalls under reduced G; Negative G; Spinning; Take-off and climb on the winch; Winch launch failures; Climb on aerotow; Take-off on aerotow; Using the airbrakes; Approach and landing; Circuit planning; Circuits without altimeter; Circuits in high winds; Cross-wind take-off and landing; Approach from awkward position; Rules and regulations; Theory. Quite a lot to get through!

The order of these items and very occasionally their names can vary slightly from club to club. A point that needs to be made is that training methods vary around the world. This book describes UK practices because they are the ones with which the author is most familiar, but the training syllabus and even how the clubs operate may be quite different elsewhere. In any event, if you learn to fly gliders anywhere beyond the UK, and happen to be reading this book, be prepared to be told 'that's not the way we do it here'.

8 Preparation for Flight

CENTRE OF GRAVITY (CG)

Before you fly you will definitely be asked how much you weigh. It is vital for safe and controllable flight that you and your instructor's combined weights lie within the limits that are placarded in the cockpit (see later note on the placard). Most instructors are good at judging a person's weight, but they need to ask to be sure, and for you to be safe, so don't be embarrassed or make something up. The range between the maximum and minimum allowable cockpit weights can vary considerably from glider to glider, but, generally speaking, if you are somewhere between ten and sixteen stone you will be fine. If you are lighter than about ten stone, ballast weights can and must be added. If you are too heavy, the club may look around for its lightest instructors, but if you really are very heavy indeed, or very tall, you may not fit into the cockpit, and unfortunately, that could decide whether gliding is the sport for you or not.

PUTTING ON A PARACHUTE

The parachute is a safety device that in all likelihood you will never need, but it does help to know how to use it. On one side of the parachute pack (the left if you are wearing it) there is a metal ring, known as the 'D' ring, attached to the rip-cord. When the 'D' ring is pulled a small spring-loaded drogue chute is released from the pack, and if the airflow is sufficient, this drags out the main canopy behind

it. The main chute requires some airflow in order to inflate fully, but whether it is the wind or you falling, there can be a delay of a few nail-biting seconds before this happens.

Oddly enough, glider pilots' parachutes are deployed far more often by accident than design. If you pick up the parachute by the 'D' ring or accidentally catch it on something, the drogue will spring out and the main canopy will probably follow suit, cascading in colourful nylon folds onto the ground. If there is anything more than a light breeze, it may then inflate and drag you off downwind. Clearly the parachute would have worked if you'd had to use it. Unfortunately, once it is out there is no way you can just stuff it back into the pack to use later. To do its job a parachute has first to be correctly packed by someone qualified to do so, which normally means sending it away for a few days.

When you put on a parachute for the first time either your instructor or another club pilot will help you with it and do up the straps for you. The ground rules are:

1) Don't pick up the parachute by the 'D' ring
2) Put your left arm through the left riser first – it helps prevent accidental deployment
3) Clip the parachute straps together, starting with the chest strap, then the leg straps. Do them up tightly. When you sit in the cockpit they will loosen up
4) After landing never unclip the parachute before getting

out, leaving it behind on the seat. In an emergency you may not be thinking quite straight, and you will do whatever you have always done when getting out of the cockpit. If you leave the parachute behind when you bail out you won't be able to go back for it

5) On the ground, outside the glider, remove the parachute by undoing the chest strap first, then the leg straps. Hold the right hand riser and let the parachute slide off your left shoulder first. That way you are less likely to pull the 'D' ring

6) It is a safety device so treat it well. Don't drop it on wet ground or allow it to get damp.

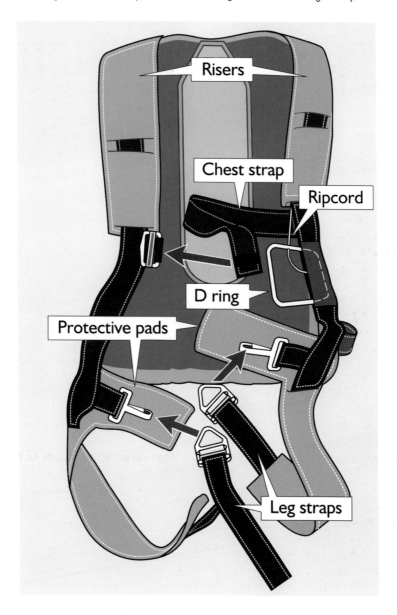

Parachute.

Using the Parachute

If you do have to use the parachute, undo the seat straps, which in most cases will mean turning a central locking buckle through about quarter of a turn. The seat strap connections vary in design so before you fly check how the ones you are using are supposed to undo – it may not be the reverse of what you did to lock them. In an emergency, pull the appropriate levers (again they vary from glider to glider) to jettison the canopy and then push it away to one side, hard. The airflow can try and hold it shut, but when it does go make sure it doesn't hit you on the head. Circumstances will determine what's possible, but go over the cockpit side and if possible fall under the wing to avoid hitting the tail assembly. Once clear of the

glider, pull the 'D' ring. Look at it before you take hold of it, just in case you accidentally grab hold of something else. Put your right thumb into the 'D', close your right hand to cover and lock the thumb, then push down on your right hand with your left, as firmly and as far as you can. Once the parachute has deployed you will find yourself gently swinging about underneath it.

During the last 50ft or so of your descent the ground will come up at a rush. A good body position is important when landing under a parachute, so get your feet and legs tight together with your feet flat to the ground and knees slightly bent. Keep your chin on your chest to avoid whiplash injury, and keep your arms as high as possible, holding the suspension lines (or steering toggles, if fitted) with your elbows in. If you are going forwards or backwards over the

Putting on a parachute.

LIMITATIONS PLACARD	BGA/267/P

B.G.A. No ...... **4840** ...... TYPE **Grob G103C Twin 2**

CATEGORY: SEMI AEROBATIC/CLOUD FLYING

SPEED LIMITATIONS (Knots)

Auto/Winch ...... **65** ...... Rough Air **92**

Aero Tow ...... **92** ...... VNE **135**

WEIGHT AND C.G LIMITATIONS

Max. Wt. (dry) **1279** ...... Max. Wt. (water) **N/A**

Empty Wt ...... **907** ...... Min. Solo. Wt **151**

Max. Solo Wt ...... **242** ...... Date Weighed ...... **28 Apr 06**

Note: Refer to Flight Manual for full limitations

Issued by .... Dated ....

COCKPIT LOADING DATA

Grob G103C Twin 2   BGA 4840

Rear Cockpit Load	Front Cockpit	
	Max	Min
0	242	151
120	242	114
140	232	107
160	212	101
180	192	100
200	172	100
220	152	100
242	130	100

Weights in pounds

Where appropriate, the limitations placard may show other detail, such as flap limiting speeds, and/or the cockpit loading limitations that apply if the glider is being flown in, say, the non-aerobatic category

Flight limitations placard for the semi-aerobatic version of the G103 Grob.

ground, rather than sideways, turn your feet so that you present the side of your leg to the direction of travel. Allow yourself to collapse progressively onto your calf and thigh, so that you lie down onto your side; don't attempt a 'stand up' landing. Any residual movement can be absorbed by rolling over, swinging your feet up and over as you go.

After touch down, release the chest clip on the parachute first, and then both thigh clips. This action is important to avoid being dragged headfirst over the ground if there is any appreciable wind. If you land in trees or get hung up in some other obstruction, don't release the harness until help arrives, as you may fall and seriously injure yourself.

THE PLACARD

The placard (see diagram above) should be attached to the cockpit wall somewhere within your view. It provides you with basic and vital information, some of which needs checking before every flight.

Category

Gliders are automatically assumed to be for soaring, and the category will indicate what else is allowed. The G103 ACRO – a fully aerobatic version of the G103C whose placard limitations are shown above – is cleared for the full range of manoeuvres, which include inverted flights, Cuban eights, flick rolls and other stomach churning antics. The overwhelming majority of gliders belong in the semi-aerobatic category; cleared for basic aerobatic manoeuvres only, which includes spins, loops, and chandelles (a posh French name for a type of wing-over). Cloud flying isn't always allowed because gliders with low drag levels at high speed – which includes most modern gliders – are rather 'slippery' and can gain speed easily and quickly if allowed to do so. The airbrakes of most gliders will prevent the speed exceeding the limit indicated by VNE (Velocity Never Exceed – see below), but only if the dive angle is no greater than 45 degrees. For some the limiting angle is only 30 degrees, which is not that steep.

SPEED LIMITATIONS

These are important. A glider is designed to withstand loads up to levels that depend to a certain extent on what it's supposed to do best. A large-span glider (22m, say) designed for cross-country flying is totally unsuitable for competition aerobatics, but a glider with a span of 15m or less, depending on what the designer intended, might be suitable – though most are not. The limiting speeds are defined by a number of closely related factors, not all of which are to do with the glider's strength.

Max. auto/winch

Even though this is the nominal maximum speed allowed on a winch or auto-tow launch, and exceeding it by small amounts is much less critical than being too slow, what doesn't appear on the placard is a minimum speed. There are two main reasons for it not being there. The first is that unlike all the other speed limitations, it has nothing to do with the glider's structural integrity. The second is that it is very dependent on the weight of the pilot(s). For example, if you and your instructor are heavy, then the minimum recommended winching speed – which is based on the unaccelerated stalling speed (see later note) times 1.5 – will be higher than if both of you are light.

Exactly how critical the maximum and minimum winch speeds are likely to be in practice depends to a very large extent on what the pilot is trying to get the glider to do at the time. We'll return to this topic later.

Max. aerotow

This is the maximum permitted speed for aerotowing. It is usually much higher than the maximum winch speed. On an aerotow the glider is being pulled from directly ahead by a rope which remains more or less in line with the fuselage and the loads on the glider are small. During a winch or auto-tow launch the cable and the glider will be at completely different angles for most of the time, pulling fairly strongly against each other, so the loads on the glider are higher.

Flaps (limiting speeds)

The limiting speeds differ for different flap settings, and it is important that they are not exceeded. In general the higher the degree of positive flap, the lower the limiting speed. (See Chapter 11 for a very brief description of what flaps do.) There may also be loading (G) limitations. These don't usually appear on the placard but will be in the glider's handbook. They may say something like 'limited to 4G with plus 35 degrees or more of positive flap'. Since the majority of gliders don't have flaps this part of the placard is usually N/A (not applicable).

Max. rough air

Broadly speaking if you are flying along and keep leaving the seat, then the air is rough. If the air is rough then you shouldn't be flying faster than the placarded maximum rough air speed. The faster you fly in rough air above this speed the more likely the glider is to suffer structural damage. There are also limits to the size of any control inputs you should make above a speed referred to as the maximum manoeuvring speed. This doesn't appear on some placards, but its value is usually fairly close to the maximum rough air speed. Above either of these speeds do not whack the controls about to the limits of their travel. There is no harm in exceeding maximum rough air if the air isn't rough, and your control movements are small and smooth, but see VNE below!

VNE (Velocity Never Exceed)

Never exceed this speed, ever. It's not just because the glider's structure may be compromised – you can apply huge and destructive loads to it at very high speeds if you are ham-fisted or just get hit by a sufficiently strong gust. It is also because a short way beyond VNE the control surfaces can suddenly begin oscillating violently and uncontrollably. This is known as 'flutter'. Once beyond VNE, any part of the glider can flutter, but it is most likely to be the control surfaces, which may then break off. Though this will give you a legitimate opportunity to try out the parachute, the situation is best avoided.

Limiting speed, gear (undercarriage) down

The most likely reason for any limit being indicated here is that the undercarriage doors could be torn off at higher speeds. This is inconvenient but not life threatening.

WEIGHT AND CG LIMITATIONS

These were mentioned earlier, but it is worth mentioning again because of their importance. The cockpit weights are calculated so that the glider's centre of gravity remains within limits which ensure that at all normal speeds the elevator remains effective – in other words, that the pilot has some control of the attitude and speed. If your weight were well below the minimum cockpit weight, then the glider's centre of gravity, where the weight is acting downwards, would be well behind the centre of the aerodynamic forces, which are generally acting upwards. The most likely result of this is that the glider will keep trying to pitch nose up, and even with the stick fully forward you may find that you can't lower it again or prevent it continuing to rise. Unfortunately this problem won't be obvious until just after you've taken off, and if you stall then, or later, as you almost certainly will, you won't have much influence on the outcome.

Maximum all up weight and empty weight

The empty weight is ascertained by weighing, but the maximum all up weight (Max AUW) is set by the designers and is related largely, but not entirely, to the glider's strength.

Maximum and minimum solo weights

For reasons already explained, never fly a glider with the cockpit weight below the minimum. If the cockpit weights are too high it may be impossible to fly the glider at a normal speed because the elevator won't hold the required attitude. The glider is not stalled (see later notes) but the elevator simply cannot cope. This can lead to problems on landing.

Maximum weight with water

Many modern gliders have provision for the addition of water ballast, often large amounts of it, in bags or tanks in

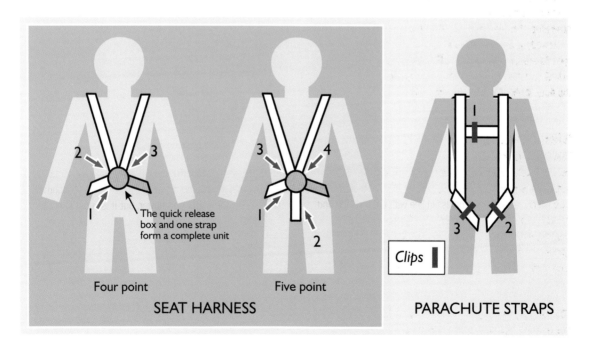

Seat and parachute harness.

the wings. Water ballast is used to shift the best glide ratio to a higher speed so that on a 'good day' when the thermals are strong, faster cross country speeds are possible (see Chapters 11 and 12). You can think of the water as adding a bit of extra horsepower to the gravity driven 'engine' described earlier. If you land at all heavily with water on board, and/or the ground run is particularly rough, the bending loads on the wings are increased hugely, the wings can start oscillating up and down ever more strongly, and the undercarriage can collapse: water is therefore normally dumped before landing. What is slightly odd about this limitation is that you would expect the take-off to create the same problems, but apparently not.

Getting in and strapping in

Before getting into the glider, check the weight limitations. If you and your instructor are below the minimum, extra ballast will be needed, and it is easier to fit this when you are out of the glider. Most two-seat gliders have special attachment points for lead or iron weights, but if you need more you may have to sit on additional weights – usually flat sheets of lead in a canvas case. Make absolutely sure that these extra weights are properly secured and can't move forward and restrict movement of the stick.

Step on the centre of the seat when you get in, not on an edge, and try not to steady yourself using the canopy. Let yourself down into the seat, placing a leg on each side of the stick as you do so. Once sat down, make sure that you are reasonably comfortable and can reach, without stretching, all knobs and levers, and the instrument panel. Anything which is mildly but noticeably uncomfortable at the start of a flight can become an unbearable instrument of torture within a few minutes. Your discomfort may end up being the only thing occupying your mind, and hence become a safety problem. Major in-cockpit adjustments are best made before take-off if only because some of them can't be made in flight. Always adjust the rudder pedals so that when you put on full rudder one way or the other your forward leg is still bent slightly at the knee, otherwise you will find the stick movement towards the extended leg will be restricted. Check that you can get the stick fully forward without your arm being completely straight. When that's all sorted, strap yourself in.

The majority of seat harnesses in gliders are four-point harnesses, ie four straps anchored to four points on the glider. The basic set-up is two lap straps and two shoulder straps. Fully aerobatic gliders have five-point harnesses with the fifth strap between your legs (see diagram on previous page). There are several different types of strap connection in use, but in whatever way they lock together, tighten up the lap-strap (the one across your midriff) first, and ensure that the buckle or connection box is in the middle. Then connect and tighten the lower centre strap, if there is one, followed by the shoulder straps – which you may have to cross over in front of you to stop them falling off your shoulders. Ensure all straps are tight, but not excessively so on the shoulders.

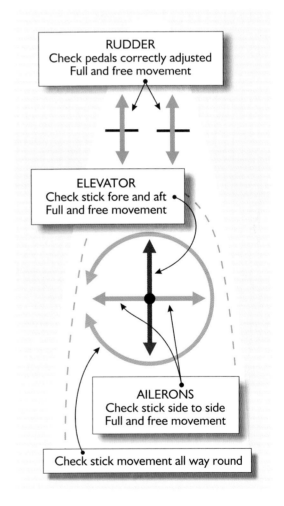

Checking the controls for full and free movement.

PRE-FLIGHT CHECKS

Some of the items in the pre-flight checks have been mentioned in some detail already and are not repeated here. The standard mnemonic is CB SIFT CBE. Each letter stands for something that must be done before take off. A problem with all check-lists is that spoken often enough the words can end up being said without anything actually being done about them. Up in the air is not the place to discover that the glider is handling badly because you are below the placarded minimum weight.

It is usual to get in, adjust the rudder pedals and then strap yourself in before doing the checks. In some gliders each rudder pedal may, for mechanical convenience, have a separate adjuster. If so, make sure that both are adjusted by the same amount. Check that you can reach everything that you need to reach, for example flap lever, panel switches and the undercarriage lever if there is one. Don't do anything with this lever unless you want the glider to sit down hard.

Controls – moving in the correct sense

Normally the controls are checked as part of the DI, and during 'positive control checks' to make sure they're actually connected, but you still have to check them before you take off. The 'moving in the correct sense' check is best done just before you get into the glider – that way you can see for yourself how the ailerons react when, for example, you move the stick to the left. In this instance the 'correct sense' means that the aileron you move the stick towards should go up (that is, the left one), and the other down. It can help to do the check facing in the same general direction as you would be when flying, towards the nose. The elevator check is straightforward, but the rudder's a bit awkward because you have to bend down and press each pedal in turn with your hands.

Full and free movement

After you've strapped yourself in, and without whacking things about and bruising the knees of your instructor, move the stick smoothly fully forwards and back, fully left and right, and then all the way round the quadrant. Check that you can get full rudder, left and right, both with and without left and right stick. Check the rudder pedals independently, again making sure that the left pedal goes forward the same distance as did the right, and vice versa. If you notice anything unusual – let's say that you can't get the stick fully back – don't even think about taking off, but find out what's causing the problem.

Ballast

This check was described earlier and ought to be done before you get in. Repeating it here is for confirmation that the cockpit weights are within limits, and any ballast is properly secured.

Straps

Make sure that straps are always done up tightly, and be sure to ask the instructor if his or hers are secure.

Instruments

Check there is no broken glass in any of the instruments. As previously described, most measure pressure in one way or another, and broken glass can amount to a puncture and either stop them working completely or cause them to misread. Gliders can be flown without the use of any instruments, but it is not a good idea to launch without at least a working ASI. Set the altimeter to zero. Gliders do not vibrate like powered aircraft, so their altimeters tend to stick. Tap the panel next to the instrument, not the glass, to unstick them. Make any adjustments necessary, and tap again – you will probably never get it to read exactly zero. Check that the ASI reads something sensible. If it says 60kt and you haven't even moved it may be broken, or the pitot or static are blocked. Be aware that while the glider is on the ground strong cross-winds blowing across the pitot pot can cause the ASI to read backwards. Reset the G meter, remembering that on the ground the 'zero' point is one (1G). Check that anything that is electric or electronic which needs to be on, such as a radio or variometer, is switched on and working. Don't play about with switches or the clear vision panel on the left of the canopy while on the launch because they'll distract you from what you ought to be concentrating on.

Flaps

If the glider has flaps set them to the correct angle for take-off. It is likely that the flap settings for aerotow and winch take-off may differ, and either may need to be adjusted during the take-off run, so remind yourself of the procedure.

Trim (green lever)

The function of the trimmer is described elsewhere, but it will determine the stick loads during the launch, as it does throughout the flight. The trimmer is usually set to neutral or slightly forward of neutral for a winch launch, and further forward for an aerotow. Some trimmers are very effective, so if you haven't trimmed the glider correctly there can be unusual or high stick loads during the launch.

Canopy (red lever) [be careful, pulling some red lever(s) will jettison the canopy]

The design of canopy locks varies quite a bit, so check that in whatever way they work they have actually engaged. Gliders like the K21 usually have an interlock between the front and rear canopies which prevents the pilot in the front seat from locking his shut until the rear canopy has been locked down.

Don't let canopies drop shut, as they can be damaged. The canopy of a glider such as the Puchacz may have an instrument panel attached and will be heavy. Never raise or lower a canopy by using the very convenient edges of the clear vision panel – it is not designed to be a handle. After you've closed and locked the canopy, push up gently on it, above your head, just to make sure. Check where the canopy jettison levers are.

Brakes

Open the airbrakes fully; check visually that left and right airbrakes are out above the wing by the same amount. Half close them. Check again, then fully close them and make sure that they are locked. The majority of glider airbrakes have over-the-centre locks, and depending on how these have been adjusted, they can sometimes be difficult to

engage. If the airbrake lever fails to 'snap' forward with a satisfying clunk, then either the brakes haven't locked or, less likely, the lock is too weak and needs adjusting. If the airbrakes aren't locked they can be bounced open on the ground run, deploy when you put any load on the glider, or just suck fully open when the speed goes above a certain value, and very likely at the least opportune moment from your point of view.

Eventualities

This is the point where you check that having previously put your brain in gear it is now fully warmed up and ready to go. Check that where you'll be going, both on the ground and in the air, isn't obstructed, take account of the wind strength and direction, and remind yourself of your nominated approach speed (see later note) just in case there is a rope or cable break; think what you will do if you have one at various heights. Will you turn left or right, or simply land ahead? Look around for other gliders. You can't see directly behind you, so you have to rely on the wingtip holder for the all clear.

You are now ready to hook on and be launched.

IN-FLIGHT CHECKS

The HASSLL check

Before any manoeuvre or sequence of manoeuvres likely to involve large and rapid changes in height, such as spins or loops, do the HASSLL checks.

Height

Check that there is sufficient height for the exercise (allow for hills) and that after it there will be enough left to enable you to get back to the airfield (easily, not just about).

Airframe

Remind yourself of the speed limitations. Check the placard. Check the canopy is closed and locked, as are the airbrakes. This last check probably sounds redundant because you have done it already before take-off. Nevertheless, do it again because it is possible that during a particularly bumpy ground run anything which can lock may partially unlock. You don't want the canopy to fly off or the airbrakes to open of their own accord. If the glider has flaps, check they are correctly set.

Straps

Check that they are tight and not likely to come undone.

Security

Make sure that there aren't any loose objects in the cockpit. Doing a reduced G exercise and watching the logbook float up in front of your face is absolutely fascinating, but distracting.

Location (ABCD)

Check that you are clear of Airfields, Built up areas, Controlled airspace and any Danger areas.

Lookout

Make a clearing S turn to look out for other aircraft, particularly below and/or approaching the airspace you are about to use. Don't do a complete 360 degree turn; other gliders may think that you are in lifting air and will come and join you.

PRE-CIRCUIT CHECKS

The checks listed below are done just prior to entering the circuit and are about the shortest set possible. There are far more elaborate pre-landing rituals upon which a club may insist. It has to be said that most training two-seaters have none of the items mentioned in the checks below, so the whole exercise can seem a bit pointless. There are varying views on the worth of pre-circuit checks anyway, but if you do one, make sure it isn't just an empty-headed recitation.

Water

Jettison any water ballast.

Undercarriage

If the glider has a retractable undercarriage, make sure it is down and locked.

Flaps

Set the flaps if there are any to an appropriate setting.

Much of what has been described so far will have sounded very procedural and rather boring, but the checks are there to make sure you haven't forgotten anything crucial to having a safe flight – that is, one that gives you the opportunity to have many more. This requires an aeroplane that is working properly, and a pilot who at least aspires to the same standard.

9 The Flight Exercises

You are now ready to fly. This chapter describes most of the exercises in the flying syllabus, but starts with one of the first and most important things you will be taught – how to keep a good lookout.

LOOKOUT

Lookout is vital to safe flight. It needs practice largely because we aren't really 'designed' to be up in the air. Our field of vision is far smaller than most birds, our sharpest visual resolution much less acute and limited to a smaller arc, and our eyes work best at close range. In addition, most of the visual cues which we use for what might be termed 'hand to hand' fighting on the ground, are absent in the air. In any event, aircraft more than a few miles away are not always the easiest things to spot, particularly if they are either on or just below the horizon. If they are on a collision course they stay in the same position relative to us and just get bigger, but this increase in size doesn't become really noticeable until they are already quite close. So if you aren't looking in the right general direction at the right moment you may not notice anything. If the object is fast-moving that can mean even less time for identifying the nature and seriousness of the threat, working out the best avoiding action and then getting the glider to do it.

Any scanning pattern must obviously take in the surroundings, but should include a check on the attitude and

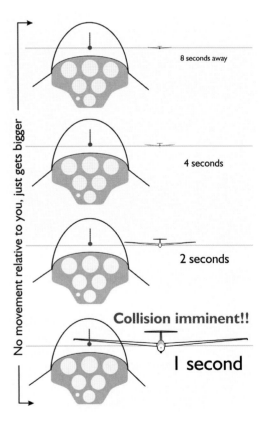

Head-on collision. Very high closing speeds.

8 seconds away

4 seconds

2 seconds

Collision imminent!!

1 second

No movement relative to you, just gets bigger

a quick cross check with the ASI. The vario may need a look unless an audio unit is attached. You might need to check the altimeter. A scan starts with the view ahead. You focus on the far horizon for a second or two, looking above and below it, and then shift your gaze to another point, say 30 to 45 degrees to the left or right, and repeat the actions.Once you've looked back as far as you can, you first look up, and then, starting with straight ahead again, look to the side opposite the one you've just covered, using the same pattern.

The chief problem with specifying any angle between each 'stop and look' point is that the smaller it is, the longer it takes to do a complete scan. Given the limitations of human vision there is a rather uncomfortable trade-off here between seeing the detail and, because a lot can change in a minute, covering the full observable area within a sensible time. We are obliged to rely heavily on our peripheral vision – which is very sensitive to movement, though not to detail (you'll see something move but you won't know what it is until you look straight at it) – to alert us to any possible threats.

You need to look initially back and away from the direction of any proposed turn to ensure that you aren't going to swing round and place a conflicting aircraft directly behind you, where you can't see it. The next step is to check the attitude and the ASI (briefly), then to shift the circle of highest priority lookout in the direction of the turn, checking that there is nothing else there. That done, initiate the turn. Once established, check the attitude regularly as part of the general scan and try to avoid looking down the inner wing or into the turn for too long as this will make speed control more difficult.

All aircraft have blind spots, and given that gliders are often circling in close proximity to each other, it is generally a good idea to try and keep the nearest more or less constantly in view and make sure that you are placed such that they can also see you. Tailgating other gliders is as rude and dangerous in the air as it is on the road.

Develop the lookout habit early on, as it becomes increasingly difficult to develop the later you leave it in your training.

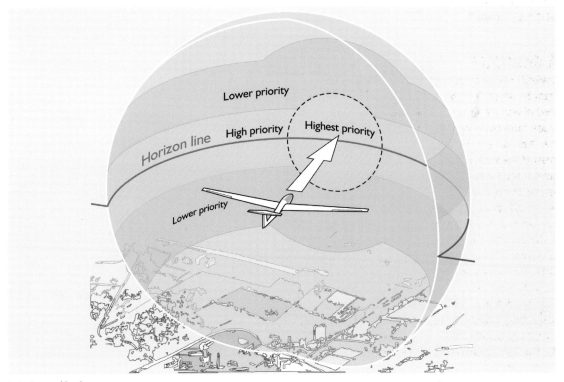

Priority and lookout.

RULES OF THE AIR

Every aviator must know this Highway Code of the air, which is a set of simple rules for dealing with likely conflict situations. There are some additional rules, dealt with later, which are specific to gliding, and cover thermalling and ridge/wave flying. The basic set is stated below as they appear in the BGA's Laws and Rules for Glider Pilots:

A glider [or any aircraft] shall not be operated in a negligent or reckless manner so as to endanger life or property, nor flown in such proximity to another as to create danger of collision, nor in formation without prior agreement of both pilots

Converging. When two aircraft are converging at approximately the same altitude, the aircraft which has the other on its right shall give way

Head-on. When two aircraft are approaching each other head-on, or approximately so, each shall alter course to the right

Overtaking. Overtaking aircraft shall at all times keep out of the way of the aircraft which is being overtaken by altering course to the right, provided that a glider overtaking another glider in the UK may alter its course to the right or the left (eg, when flying on a ridge).

Whereas aeroplanes shall when converging give way to aerotows and gliders shall give way to balloons, it is nevertheless the responsibility of all glider pilots at all times to take all possible measures to avoid collision.

The last paragraph hints, rather heavily, that though aeroplanes are legally obliged to give way to gliders, don't bet on it.

Note that in the converging case illustrated opposite the glider which has to give way has been depicted as turning to pass behind the other glider. Circumstances may alter what's actually required, or even possible, but in general if you do have to take avoiding action it is best if it ends with the other aircraft going away from you, and preferably in the opposite direction.

Winter aerotow take-off.

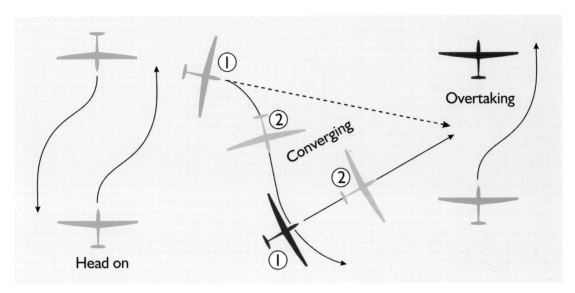

Rules of the air (general).

PRIMARY AND FURTHER (SECONDARY) EFFECTS OF THE CONTROLS

The very first pre-flight briefings and demonstrations will be about the controls, what they do and their primary and further effects – all dealt with earlier in Chapter 3, 'How Gliders Work'.

USE OF THE TRIMMER

The trimmer can be thought of as a work-load control – specifically reducing the effort needed to control speed – so its use is introduced very early on. How it works is easiest to describe by way of an example.

As you will be shown during your first few flights, gliders have some inherent stability. Practically speaking the result is that if you let go of the stick the glider will fly steadily hands-off at say, 50kt. To fly it at 60kt you will have to keep a constant forward pressure on the stick because the glider will be trying to return to the 50kt attitude. The faster you wish to go the greater the forward pressure required. Likewise, if 40kt was your preferred speed, then you would have to maintain a constant back pressure. Having to fight the glider in this way can get very tiring and makes accurate speed control more difficult. The

trimmer removes the stick loads by altering the position of the elevator slightly (this is what you were having to do) and changes the 'hands-off' speed.

There are two main types of trimmer, aerodynamic and spring. Aerodynamic trimmers, illustrated overleaf, are like small elevators on the elevator. The simplest type moves the tab either up or down in response to the (green) trim lever in the cockpit. Moving the trim lever forwards raises the tab, which then pushes the elevator down and vice versa. There are a number of variations on this simple set-up, one of which is designed to increase the stick loads when the elevator is deflected. Tabs with this additional function can be seen on gliders like K13s. Spring trimmers tend to be a bit 'woolly' in their action by comparison to aerodynamic trimmers, and are usually out of sight, attached to the elevator push rod below the pilot's seat. Aerodynamic trimmers create extra drag. Spring trimmers do not, at least directly, so the majority of modern gliders have spring trimmers.

To set the trimmer, first stabilize and hold the attitude and speed you want. Move the trim lever in the same direction as you are putting pressure on the stick, eg trim forward if you are having to push and vice versa. At one particular position of the trim lever the stick loads will disappear. The glider should now fly hands–off at the chosen speed, and if you try and fly at any other speed you

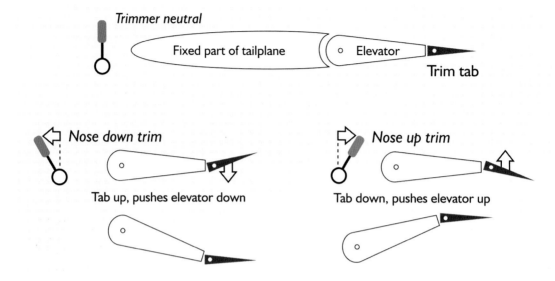

Aerodynamic trim tab.

will again have to apply a constant forward or backward pressure on the stick.

In general, trim the glider for any new attitude/speed that is going to last longer than a few seconds. Never take your hands off the stick if the glider is seriously out of trim, and be cautious about taking them off even when you believe it to be in trim.

Straight flight – speed control

Controlling the speed is relatively straight-forward to describe, if not initially to do. You look out ahead, see where the horizon is in relation to the nose or the top edge of the cockpit or panel and check the ASI. If the ASI is steady at the chosen speed, maintain the position of the nose in relation to the horizon (attitude again) by appropriate use of the elevator. If you get into a different glider the attitude for any given speed will look different, so you need to check it against the ASI.

Ignoring the ASI indications for the moment, clues to the speed are:

• Attitude, which only works reliably in free flight (ie not on the launch)
• The general noise level (extremely low in modern gliders)

• And sometimes, but not always: the feel of the controls. They tend to be rather sloppy and unresponsive at very low speeds.

Aerodynamic trim tab on the Puchacz.

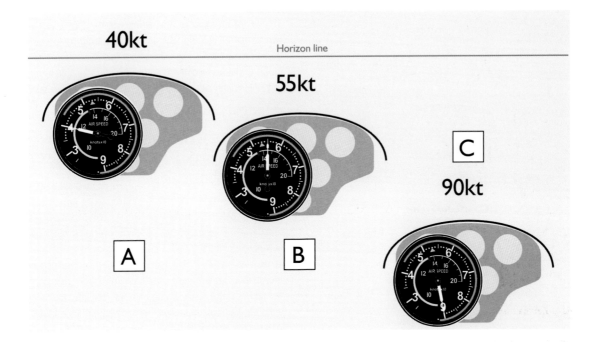

Relationship between attitude and airspeed.

The views A, B and C in the diagram above represent the attitudes and related steady speeds of an anonymous glider. If our chosen speed is 55kt, then the related attitude is B, let's say. Regardless of the speed beforehand, if you use the elevator to lower the nose from position A to B, or raise it from position C to B, after a short while the speed will stabilize at 55kt. Likewise if you go from A to C or B to C, the speed will always end up at 90kt.

Using attitude to control the speed rather than the ASI has big advantages. If the glider is going at a steady speed and you lower the nose to a new attitude, it takes time to accelerate to the new speed. Small changes in attitude are relatively easy to detect, so if air movement causes the nose to rise or drop slightly from, for example, attitude B, the elevator can be used to return the glider to B before it has had time to accelerate or decelerate much, if at all.

You have to monitor the ASI during a launch and the approach and landing, but for most other phases of flight, relying on attitude and cross checking occasionally with the ASI is best. If you use the ASI by itself you will react to speed changes only when the ASI registers them, and that will put you slightly behind what's actually happening. It isn't the ASI that is lagging, but the glider, so you will tend to overshoot your chosen speed each time and swoop up and down (usually quite gently) as you 'chase the ASI'. Your lookout will also suffer.

Using the attitude for speed control is easy if the visibility is good and there is a distinct horizon, but in bad visibility you can still check the attitude by reference to the amount of ground in view ahead and to each side. There will come a point where the visibility is so bad that it isn't legal to fly, but before then it may still be bad enough to cause disorientation, and in those circumstances it is arguable whether beginners can learn anything useful. Your instructor may well suggest you don't fly.

Straight flight – wings level

For straight flight the view ahead needs to be symmetrical. If the wings are not level by even the smallest degree, the glider will try to turn in the direction of the lower wing. Initially it will be difficult to detect very small angles of bank, and you will probably counteract any gradual drift of the nose to left or right by applying a small amount of

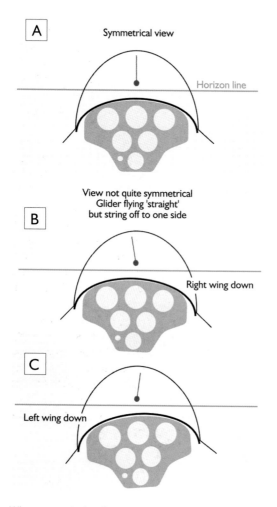

A
Symmetrical view

Horizon line

B
View not quite symmetrical
Glider flying 'straight'
but string off to one side

Right wing down

C
Left wing down

Wings not quite level.

opposite rudder. This looks as though it has fixed the problem, but although the glider is now flying straight, it is doing so sideways and with crossed controls (eg left rudder and right aileron). The clue is that even though the glider isn't turning, the string is pointing off to one side (see diagram above). If you try to get the string 'in the middle' (blowing straight towards you) by correcting with rudder alone, the glider will then do what it was trying to do all along, which is to turn. If that's not what you want, level the wings using a small amount of aileron and co-ordinate it with appropriate and small amounts of rudder. Easily said, difficult to do.

A word of warning. The string will be only a foot or two ahead of you, so focusing on it will blur everything that's further away and affect your lookout. When trying to co-ordinate the controls (see below), feel what the glider is doing and use the string out of the corner of your eye.

CO-ORDINATION AND BALANCED FLIGHT

Co-ordination is about flying the glider without slipping or skidding sideways, a condition referred to as 'unbalanced flight'. To keep the wings level or to bank to turn, you must use the ailerons, but perversely, if used by them-selves, they put the glider into unbalanced flight which, apart from anything else, increases the drag and reduces the glider's performance. Adverse yaw (glider rolls right but initially the nose swings off to the left, and vice versa) is particularly bad at low speeds, but even though it becomes less evident the faster you go, it never disap-pears entirely. To counteract it you need to use the stick and rudder together; left rudder with left stick and right rudder with right stick. The exact amount of rudder required depends on how much aileron has been applied and how quickly, varies also with the speed and indeed with the type of glider – generally speaking the longer the span the worse the effect. Both the string and the T/S ball are invaluable aids to maintaining balanced, non-slipping, non-skidding flight, but the string is by far the most sensitive and because it's usually right in front of you, you don't have to look down into the cockpit as you must with the T/S ball.

TURNING

For reasons that are not at all obvious, turning can often be a lot easier than flying in a straight line. In order to turn you must bank the glider so that some of the lift from the wings will pull (accelerate) the glider in the direction in which you wish to go. The wing must create more lift so that it can continue to support the glider's weight and provide the required into-turn force. The quicker the required change in direction, the steeper the bank will need to be and the more lift the wing will have to produce.

Medium turns

Having had a good look round, check the attitude and speed and then, with co-ordinated aileron and rudder, roll the glider smoothly and positively into the turn. You will need a gentle backward pressure on the stick at the same time to prevent the nose dropping. Try to keep your body upright in relation to the glider; go with it, and don't lean into or out of the turn.

If you fly largely by attitude, which is preferable, you'll almost certainly have chosen a pitch reference point on, say, the top centre of the instrument panel (black Xs in the figure). Neither this point nor your head will necessarily be on the axis around which the glider rolls, and when you go into a turn it can look as if the pitch attitude is changing even when it isn't. In balanced flight, turning or not, it is the vertical distance between the red X (picture below) and the horizon that determines the glider's speed, not black X. What the picture actually looks like for varying degrees of bank, and how closely you have to monitor attitude and airspeed, depends very much on seating position and panel shape, but in modern gliders your eye-line is usually quite close to the rolling axis, if not precisely on it. The problem only becomes really obvious when you try to do a well balanced and steady airspeed turn in a side-by-side two-seater – rare beasts these days – where black X can drop way below the horizon when you're on the inside of the turn, and be on or above it when you're on the outside. Once the desired angle of bank is reached, centralise the ailerons, though a small amount of out of turn aileron may be required to prevent the bank increasing. If you need a large amount and are having to move the stick well back to maintain the attitude, then something else may be about to happen (see spinning). With the stick central or nearly so, some into-turn rudder may still be required for balanced flight, but far less than was needed to co-ordinate the initial roll into the turn.

While turning, take note of any sensations you have of sliding sideways on the seat, either into or out of the turn. They are fairly subtle, unless you are flying very badly, and if you are tense you probably won't notice them. If you do, they are very useful background clues to whether the turn is balanced or not. If the glider is slipping into the turn you will feel as if you are sliding in that direction. If it is skidding out of the turn you will feel yourself sliding towards the raised wing. Make any adjustments necessary, remembering that changing the amount of rudder, for example, will have other effects that you will then need to correct.

Assuming adequate speed, if you move the stick to the left and the nose yaws to the right with the string streaming in the same direction, then you aren't using enough rudder. If you use too much rudder when initiating say, a left turn, or use the rudder too soon (which amounts to the same thing), then the nose will swing left fairly swiftly and the string will stream left, indicating that the glider is skidding out of the intended turn.

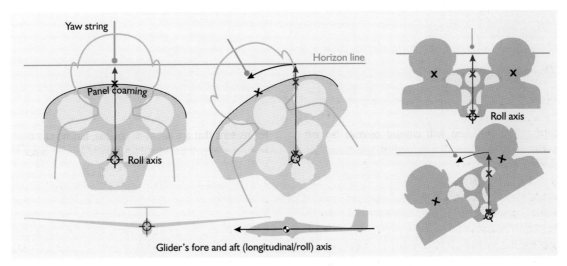

Apparent changes in pitch attitude during a turn.

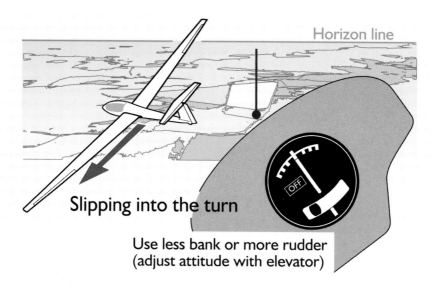

Horizon line

Slipping into the turn

Use less bank or more rudder
(adjust attitude with elevator)

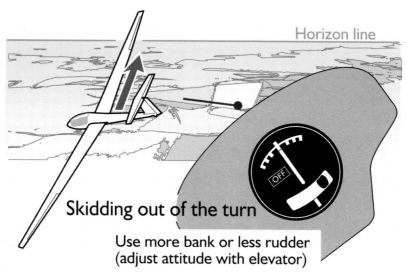

Horizon line

Skidding out of the turn

Use more bank or less rudder
(adjust attitude with elevator)

Slipping and skidding.

To help improve your co-ordination you will be asked to roll out of your turn onto specific headings. Your instructor may say 'turn left and come out heading directly towards that lake' or something similar. Remember that as long as the glider is banked it will continue to turn. Glider rates of roll can be quite slow, so you need to anticipate and start rolling level shortly before you reach the desired heading.

Steep or tight turns

You will tackle these later in your training because they are more difficult to do – speed control is the main problem. The steeper the bank the more work the wing must do to provide both the into-turn force and the component supporting the weight. At 90 degrees of bank it doesn't matter how hard the wing works because even if it could produce an infinite amount of lift none of it would be

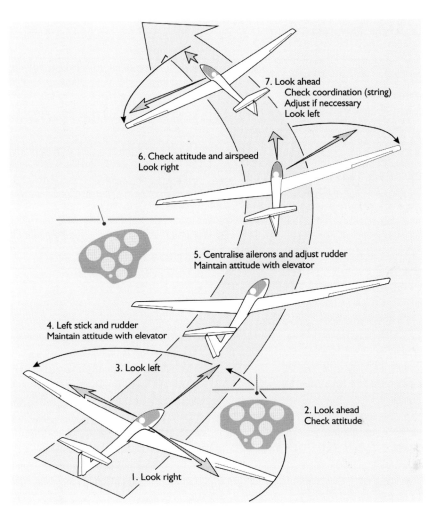

7. Look ahead
   Check coordination (string)
   Adjust if neccessary
   Look left

6. Check attitude and airspeed
   Look right

5. Centralise ailerons and adjust rudder
   Maintain attitude with elevator

4. Left stick and rudder
   Maintain attitude with elevator

3. Look left

2. Look ahead
   Check attitude

I. Look right

Entering a turn.

supporting the vertical component of the glider's weight (see illustration on page 33). The result is that the glider will go into a huge sideslip. Typically you will be taught steep turns of about 60 degrees to 70 degrees of bank.

First increase the airspeed above the normal flying speed by about 10kt. Check the attitude; lookout and then roll smoothly into a steeply banked turn. More back pressure on the stick is needed than before to prevent the speed building. If the speed does start to increase, trying to slow down by raising the nose with the elevator will only make the turn even tighter, so you need to reduce the bank first. Check and stabilize the attitude and speed, then roll into the steeper bank again. As you roll out of the turn

remember to relax the back pressure on the stick, otherwise the nose will pitch up above the horizon.

Your instructor may ask you to practice keeping the speed constant while rolling from a tight turn in one direction to another. Again, pay attention to attitude and co-ordination, and don't forget the lookout. Generally you need more rudder to start the roll and reduce it once the glider is rolling, so some nifty footwork is required. The exercise is quite difficult and can require a fair amount of physical effort because of higher control loads. Incidentally, make sure you are tightly strapped in, otherwise your strenuous efforts on the controls may have more effect on where you are sitting on the seat than on what the glider does.

STALLING AND SPINNING

Why you have to do stalling and spinning exercises

As described in Chapter 3, when the wing/aerofoil is being asked to produce more lift than is possible in the circumstances, it stalls. Providing the glider is flying within the placarded weight limits, the glider will behave at the stall in a largely predictable way, as it was designed to do. Just before the stall there will be characteristic warning symptoms that the AoA is too high. These will include some but not necessarily all of the following:

• Nose attitude higher than normal
• Slow or reducing airspeed
• Changes in the volume and/or character of the airflow noise (for example, what was previously a gentle hiss may become a loud whooshing sound – depends a bit on the glider)
• Flickering of the ASI
• Buffet (the stick and/or the whole glider shakes)
• Lack of, or changes in the effectiveness of the elevator, ailerons and/or rudder
• Unusual positions of the controls for the phase of flight (e.g. lots of aileron away from the direction of a turn)
• Higher rate of descent

The one infallible clue to stalling is that pulling back on the stick won't raise the nose. Some of the other symptoms can occur when the glider isn't stalled, or even anywhere near it. For example, buffet can occur when the airbrakes are out, and the ASI can flicker if there is water in the pitot tube.

Spinning occurs when one wing stalls before the other, due either to yaw being present or misuse of the ailerons. The glider rolls towards the stalled wing and enters into a vertically descending spiral, losing height fast, and simultaneously rolling, pitching and yawing. It is an unfortunate fact of life that every aeroplane currently in use, bar a very few, will stall and spin, some more readily than others, and that 99.9 per cent of the time the pilot is the cause. Four points about stalling and spinning in relation to gliders need noting:

1) Gliders spend a significant part of their flying time quite close to the stall

2) Stalling and spinning are easy to avoid if you recognize the symptoms
3) Doing either low down, spinning in particular, is asking for trouble
4) If the glider does stall and/or spin, you must take the correct recovery action

The chief problem with both, but in particular spinning, is that the untutored and automatic reaction to the situation is virtually guaranteed to ensure that it doesn't change, or gets worse, so training and practice in these exercises are vital.

Demos that don't work

Deliberate stalls and spins are not usually a problem, given sufficient height; but accidental ones, where the pilot fails to realize what has happened, are potentially far more serious. Because of this there is a fairly heavy emphasis during the training on learning about stalling and spinning. Occasionally, a demonstration involving either may not work; perhaps the glider didn't spin when the instructor thought it would, or it couldn't be made to spin at all. Some training gliders are hard to spin, but most single-seat gliders do so fairly easily. In any event, you will be told what ought to have happened. Never assume from failed demonstrations that the risks don't exist or are too small to bother about. Such conclusions are far more risky than the exercises, startling as a few of them may be. Despite the fact that some of them may sound fairly hair-raising, think of them as worthwhile life insurance, because that's what they are.

THE STRAIGHT, UNACCELERATED (NORMAL) STALL

The initial exercises are designed to give you some appreciation of the various symptoms of a high AoA (see Chapter 3), and to demonstrate that if the glider stalls you cannot raise the nose, indeed it may drop, even with the stick fully back. The first exercise will be a straight and unaccelerated stall; referred to as such because the loading throughout is supposed to stay near enough 1G. Having done the HASSLL checks the instructor will increase the speed slightly, and then gradually and smoothly raise the nose so that as the

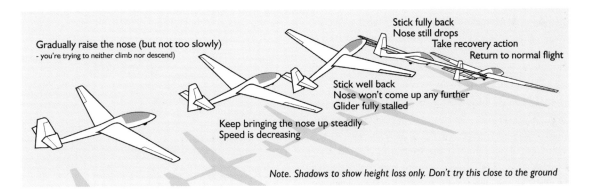

Gradually raise the nose (but not too slowly)
- you're trying to neither climb nor descend)

Stick fully back
Nose still drops
Take recovery action
Return to normal flight

Stick well back
Nose won't come up any further
Glider fully stalled

Keep bringing the nose up steadily
Speed is decreasing

Note. Shadows to show height loss only. Don't try this close to the ground

Straight and unaccelerated stall.

glider decelerates it remains in more or less level flight. To keep the nose coming up the stick will have to come further and further back, but at some point, even with full up elevator, the nose will drop of its own accord. The glider has stalled. Make a note of the airspeed at which this occurs. It does vary slightly, depending on the instructor's technique, but keep that speed in mind for comparison with its value during some of the other exercises.

Stall recovery

The recovery is straightforward. Since the stall was caused by too high an AoA, the first thing to do is to reduce it. Ease the stick forward and lower the nose to below the normal flying attitude. Once the speed is adequate, recover smoothly to normal flight.

Virtually every other stalling and spinning exercise can be regarded as an elaboration of the original straight stall, encompassing those where the glider is manoeuvring and the loads are higher than normal – sometimes lower – or those where one wing stalls before the other, which can lead to a spin.

Wing drop

The straight stall is supposed to be just that, but if there is any yaw present or the ailerons are deflected, then the glider will probably 'drop a wing', indicating that one wing stalled fractionally before the other. The wing drop is a precursor of the spin. If you try to pick up the dropping wing by using the ailerons, the aileron on the downgoing

side moves downward as well, increasing the already critical AoA and making the situation worse. If, however, you smartly centralize the ailerons and lower the nose just as the wing drop starts, both wings will unstall and the glider will end up nose down, albeit in a slightly lopsided attitude, and accelerating. Once the speed is adequate, level the wings and recover smoothly to normal flight.

Mushing stalls

If the straight stall described earlier is approached more gently the glider can end up with the nose slightly high, stalled, descending at a high rate, but with full up elevator (stick hard back) just able to prevent the nose from dropping. The only way to recover is to lower the nose first and allow the speed to increase. If you fail to do this, any attempt at turning will cause the glider to spin, probably quite suddenly.

Zero G and reduced, or negative G

Zero G is the slightly unpleasant sensation which we associate with going over a hump-backed bridge or falling over. In normal circumstances we react to a fall by pushing our hands forward to protect our heads. A tiny number of people react very strongly to any sensation of reduced G by throwing their heads back and hands forward, and occasionally becoming completely unconscious for a few seconds. If they happen to be holding the controls at the time the stick is pushed hard forward and the glider pitches violently nose down. This makes the falling sensation worse, so they push even harder. Close to the ground the results could be fatal. Provided you don't have this reaction too strongly, don't worry, you can be trained out of it, but it is very important to identify it early in your training.

At least one of the exercises will demonstrate to you the differences between being genuinely stalled, which requires the nose to be lowered to recover, and merely feeling as if you have stalled, which may require only minimal action. It is important to be able to distinguish between the two, and the distinction lies not so much in what you feel, which can mislead, but in the effectiveness of the controls. If the glider is stalled you won't be able to raise the nose and the ailerons will either be very sluggish or not work at all. If you are not stalled then all the controls will remain effective.

Scenarios – the play's the thing

For some demonstrations the instructor may describe to you a scenario more or less along the lines of 'this is how you can get into this kind of situation' followed by 'and if you then do this' – usually 'this' means failing to notice something important – 'this is what happens next'. Strange gyrations can follow. These scenarios are almost always played out high up because 'next' can involve a large loss of height.

ACCELERATED STALLS

The unaccelerated stall demonstrated some, if not all, of the symptoms of an approaching stall, but in reality you are more likely to stall when manoeuvring than when flying in a straight line. Anything larger or smaller than 1G will change the glider's effective weight and alter the stalling speed – see the table on the right. The demonstrations will emphasize the fact that whatever the airspeed, if the AoA is high enough you will stall –there is no 'maybe' or 'perhaps' about it. The order of the demonstrations and any related exercises can vary from club to club, but you will be taken through the entire sequence during the course of several flights.

High speed or accelerated stalls

Theoretically you may know that the glider can stall at any speed if you increase the load enough, but this demonstra-

'G'	Stalling speed (kt)
0	0
0.25	19
0.5	27
1 (Normal)	38 (eg)
1.1	40
1.5	46.5
2	54
3	66
5	85
10	120

Negative (above), *Positive* (below)

G (load) and changes in stalling speed.

tion will help prove it, and show that violent movements of the controls are best avoided. The instructor will first do a 'normal' unaccelerated stall as a yardstick for what will follow. After taking the appropriate recovery action, and with the nose fairly well down, the speed is allowed to build to about 15kt above the unaccelerated stall speed. This will only take a few seconds and so far, nothing very much will happen. The scenario previously painted for you might be that of an accidental stall low down, where you find yourself pointing earthwards at a steep angle and the ground uncomfortably close. The understandable reaction is to pull out as quickly as possible, and that's what the instructor does, hauling the stick to the back stop and applying full up elevator. The nose will begin to rise, maybe not very far, but the glider will continue to descend, shuddering violently and usually making a lot more noise. A wing may drop. What has happened is that even though the initial speed was well above the normal stalling speed, the pilot asked far too much of the wing and stalled it, again. Had the recovery from the first stall been less all or nothing, then the second accelerated stall would not have occurred.

In most of the stalling and spinning exercises the onset of buffeting will indicate a high AoA. For example, for the exercise called 'stall in a turn' the instructor flies a moderately banked turn and then starts to slow the glider down. At some point it will start to shudder – sometimes only the stick will shake – and if you look at the ASI you will see that the speed is higher than for the normal unaccelerated stall. Easing off the back pressure on the stick is all that's required to reduce the AoA and the buffet. The exercise may explore steeper bank angles in the same manner, demonstrating how the stalling speed creeps up as the loads increase.

SPINNING

Spin training is left until late in the syllabus, firstly because, ironically, you need to be able to fly the glider reasonably well to do something which is usually the result of bad handling, and secondly, if you're not reasonably relaxed about flight, spinning can seem a bit alarming.

The spin was described earlier, but the key point is that one wing must stall before the other. There will always be some warnings that a spin is about to occur, but if your attention is elsewhere – at least one of the exercises simulates this – you may miss them.

Spinning off cable breaks

This is something that you do NOT want to do during a real launch, particularly low down, either for practice or by accident, because at best you will give yourself a serious fright. The effect has to be simulated at a safe altitude, where it is innocuous. The demonstration aims to show you that what may look OK can, in some circumstances, be anything but OK.

The instructor will dive the glider to about 70 or 80kt, pull up into a climb at an angle similar to that of a winch launch, and wait for the speed to fall to what would be a typical winch launching speed, say 55kt. At that point he or she may mark the imaginary break by saying 'bang', and then for a split second do nothing about it, allowing for the fact that nobody's reactions are ever instantaneous – and that if you weren't expecting the break you will take longer to respond. The stick is then moved fully forward and the nose lowered to the normal flying attitude.

Two things need noting. Firstly, during most of the pitch-over the glider is decelerating, so the elevator becomes less and less effective. As a result it takes a surprisingly

long time to reach the intended attitude which, in this case, is going to be the wrong one anyway – it ought to be steeper. Secondly, you and the glider are following a more or less ballistic trajectory (rather like the one a ball will follow when thrown) and are being accelerated in the direction in which gravity is acting. The practical result is that gravity's effect will be less than normal, so you and the aeroplane don't weigh as much – you could both easily weigh nothing – and crucially, the wing has less to support. Thus, even though the airspeed is low, possibly way below the unaccelerated stalling speed, both the AoA and the stalling speed will be temporarily lower than usual. For the moment there isn't a problem. However, when the pilot stops pushing forward on the stick and moves it to hold the glider in the normal flying attitude, everything returns immediately to its normal 1G weight. If the speed is already low then the resulting AoA will be high and the glider may either then be fully stalled, or very close to it.

At this point the instructor attempts a turn, simulating a situation where you have looked ahead and decided there was insufficient space left in which to land. Even if the turn is well balanced the glider will roll rapidly in the direction of the turn, through the partially inverted position, and then enter an upright spin. You will probably be surprised at the lack of any very obvious prior warning, and the speed with which everything goes pear-shaped. Had the nose been lowered further and the speed allowed to increase significantly before the turn was initiated, then the spin wouldn't have occurred.

The exercise demonstrates the importance of having at least the approach speed before you even think about turning following a cable break (see diagram on next page). But, having said that, there is one occasion where you won't be able to lower the nose to well below the normal flying attitude, and that's if a break occurs just after take-off, close to the ground. How to deal with this is covered later under cable breaks and launch failures.

Spinning off accelerated stalls (stalls in turns)

The purpose of this demonstration is to show you the results of mishandling the controls when you are turning. Again, what will take you aback is the speed with which everything goes from more or less OK to rather less than

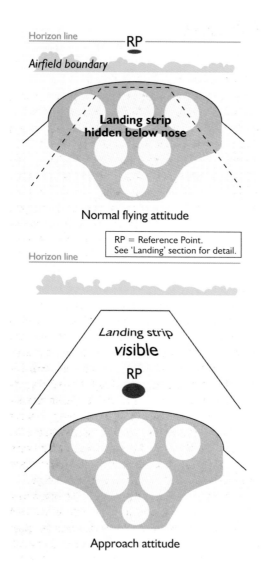

Importance of attitude after a cable break.

OK. The scenario may go something like this: you are thermalling with several other gliders and in your anxiety to keep them all in view, are paying insufficient attention to flying your glider.

The instructor will fly a fairly steep turn at about 45kt to 50kt and feed in gradually more and more rudder to keep the turn going, plus out-of-turn aileron to stop the bank increasing, and some back stick to prevent the nose

dropping. Despite the apparently safe speed the increased yaw will have an effect on the inner wing's AoA, as will the increasing amount of back stick, not to mention the position of the ailerons. At first, nothing very much seems to happen. The glider skids round the turn and is a bit noisy, which may give the false impression that you are going faster than you actually are. The major clue to subsequent events is in the control positions, but in the scenario you haven't noticed them. You're pulling more G than normal, but not much (it is, after all, supposed to be a fairly tight turn). A brief glance at the ASI shows 50kt. Suddenly the glider rolls over and goes into a spin. If this happens to you accidentally it will come as a bit of a shock. The cause? A higher than normal stalling speed because of the increased loading and extremely poor handling of the controls brought about, partly, by distraction. This doesn't mean that every time you mishandle the controls you're going to spin – nobody would ever learn to fly if that were the case – but that in the circumstances what you were doing pretty well guaranteed that you would spin, and indeed you did.

Recovery procedure for spins

Spin recovery is straightforward, but the actions must be taken in the order described:

1) Full opposite rudder – to reduce the amount of yaw and to help pitch the nose down
2) Centralise ailerons – to reduce the downgoing wing's angle of attack
3) Move the stick progressively forwards until the rotation stops. This is to unstall the glider even if the nose is already pointing steeply downwards
4) When the rotation stops, centralise the rudder – you will be steeply nose down at this point and accelerating rapidly
5) Recover smoothly from the ensuing dive

SPIRAL DIVES

The spiral dive can sometimes get confused with the spin, but they are not the same. When the glider is spiral diving all the controls work, whereas if the glider is spinning they do not. So for example, if you pull the stick back and G

Spiral dive	Spin
G increase	G remains near enough constant
Bank tends to increase	Bank stays constant but can lessen
Airspeed increases	Airspeed stays more or less constant
Initial rate of descent may be low	Rate of descent is very high
High rate of turn accompanied by high G	High rate of rotation, but may be inconsistent. The glider can pitch up and down as well as speed up and slow down as it rotates.
All the controls work	The ailerons don't work and the elevator won't raise the nose
Pulling back increases G	Pulling back has no effect

Symptoms of spiral dive and spin.

increases, that would suggest that the elevator is working. If you apply the recovery action for a spiral dive to a spin you won't recover, and if you apply spin recovery to a spiral dive you can overstress the glider, so it's important to know the differences.

The first action to take if the glider is spiral diving is to roll off at least some of the bank before pulling out. Don't roll and pull at the same time if the speed is very high since the glider can be over-stressed.

TAKING-OFF

General remarks

Most modern two-seater gliders take-off and touch down at airspeeds of around 40kt (46mph), which at altitude will seem a crawl. It will appear faster the lower you are and ridiculously fast during, say, a no-wind take-off. The sensation of excessive speed is the result of your brain working rather slowly. That's not supposed to be an insult – the human brain is poor at grasping the complete picture if it hasn't been trained to recognize it first, and in that respect familiarity will be your friend. The more take-offs you do, the more manageably slow everything will seem to become.

The ground run

After hooking on and checking that it is all clear, you are ready to launch. During the initial ground run you need to keep the wings level using the ailerons and steer using the rudder – don't bank the glider when you're on the ground. Most two-seat training gliders start with the nose wheel or skid on the ground and the tail up, though if the initial acceleration is particularly fierce the tail can bang down momentarily. No matter how fast the glider is going, it won't take-off if the nose wheel is kept on the ground, so use the elevator to raise the nose just enough to keep both the nose wheel and tail wheel clear of the ground. The glider is now 'running on the main wheel' (see diagram on next page).

The controls won't work very well until the airflow over them is sufficient. This means that in light or no wind conditions the pilot has little influence over what the glider does during the first few seconds of the ground run, though the launch cable can be released if things aren't going quite as they ought. The wingtip holder keeps the wings level during this initial stage, but there may be a short gap between them letting go – usually they simply can't run any faster – and the controls having any effect unless they are used very coarsely and promptly. If a wing touches the ground at this point, release immediately. The only real difference between the ground runs of the various launch methods is the acceleration. Winch and auto-tow accelerate the glider rapidly and the controls 'bite' sooner, unlike an aerotow, even though the slipstream from the tug's propeller can sometimes help.

Once the glider has taken off, an aerotow must be treated in a completely different manner to a winch or auto-tow launch.

THE WINCH LAUNCH

Take–off and climb

If correctly trimmed for the winch launch, with the trim set slightly forward of neutral, most training gliders will more or less take-off and rotate into the climb by themselves, but this is not guaranteed. In any event, when the speed during the ground run is sufficient the controls will begin to work positively and effectively, and shortly after that the glider will lift off. You might have to tweak the stick back to 'unstick' if the glider seems a bit reluctant to take-off, but don't just haul back until it does because the moment you're off the ground the nose will pitch up strongly. The usual reasons for failing to take-off are insufficient speed or you've held the nose down too much.

Just after take-off, don't allow the glider to rotate into a steep climb, nor rotate it yourself, if the speed is either low or not increasing. The ASI needs monitoring (brief glances only). Smoothly steepen the climb as height and speed increase. The glider should not be in the full climb attitude (about 45–50 degrees nose up) much below 300ft (see diagram on next page). There is a fine balance here. Rotate too rapidly into the climb and you can break the cable or the weak link, or, if the speed is insufficient, you can stall the glider. Rotate too slowly and you may find yourself going too fast. If it has to be one or the other, too fast is far preferable to too slow.

If the trimmer has been correctly set to start with, once the glider is in the full climb the stick loads should be low and there should be no need for you to hold the stick against the back stop. You might conceivably get a little extra height on the launch by doing so, but it's not very good practice. If the cable or weak link break – always assume they might – full up elevator will raise the nose further before you have time to react and lower it (see emergency procedures later).

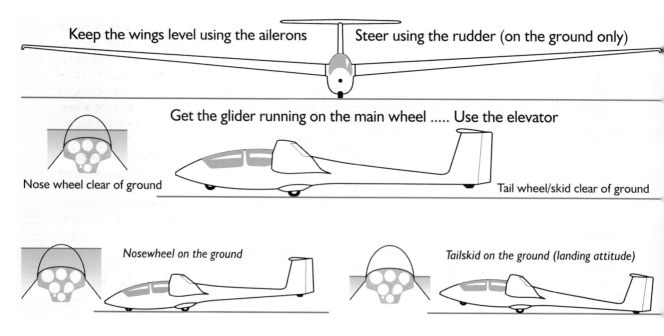

Keep the wings level using the ailerons   Steer using the rudder (on the ground only)

Get the glider running on the main wheel ..... Use the elevator

Nose wheel clear of ground   Tail wheel/skid clear of ground

Nosewheel on the ground   Tailskid on the ground (landing attitude)

The ground run.

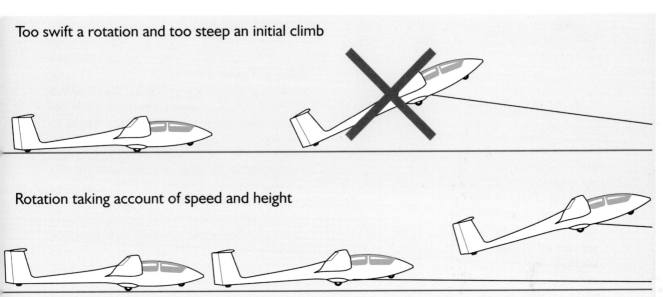

Too swift a rotation and too steep an initial climb

Rotation taking account of speed and height

Take-off and rotation into climb.

Though attitude is the key to speed in free flight, during a winch launch the speed is more in the hands of the winch driver than the pilot. By altering the attitude the pilot can to some extent control the launch speed, but a lot depends on the type of winch. For example, if you pull steeper into the climb on a low powered winch you're quite likely to slow down, whereas if you do the same with a high powered winch (depending on how the power transmission works), you will almost certainly speed up.

The glider will be winched using the belly hook and once in the climb there is no great tendency for the glider automatically to line itself up with the winch. The pilot has to see to that, but in the full climb the fuselage blocks the view downwards and forwards. The higher you go the more extensive the view sideways, but by the same token the cone of 'invisibility' beneath increases in size and can end up covering the entire airfield. If there are clouds above and ahead, choose one as a reference. You will be on the launch for about a minute, so the cloud won't have moved very far in that time. After a few launches you will be able to judge where you are in relation to the invisible winch from what you can see to each side, so you won't be thrown by cloudless days.

Releasing

Towards the top of the launch the pull of the cable will gradually lower the nose. You can't stop this happening, so don't fight it by hauling the stick onto the back stop. Some increase in the back pressure may be needed, but it depends on the glider. When you judge that you are almost over the winch, lower the nose to the normal flying attitude to take some of the tension off the cable, and then pull the release. During your first few attempts to release in the right place, the winch or auto-tow driver will probably beat you to it by reducing the power, whereupon the cable will back-release. In some clubs the approved technique is for the winch/tow car driver always to beat you to it when he judges that you're as high on the launch as you're ever going to get, or if there is any danger of the cable dropping in a heap on top of the winch/tow car.

THE AUTO-TOW LAUNCH

The take-off procedure is much the same as for a winch, though the initial acceleration may be slower and the take-off run slightly longer. The rotation into the climb is similar but the climb attitude may deliberately be less steep. One reason for this is that if the glider is pulling up against the

AEROTOWING

Take-off and climb

Aerotowing is basically formation flying. Apart from the acceleration and longer ground run mentioned earlier, the chief differences between aerotowing and other methods of launch are:

l) The position of the glider in relation to the tug is important, particularly during the first 1,200ft or so
2) Keeping station requires more concentration
3) During a tow the glider will usually be going faster than during a winch launch, so the controls are more responsive
4) The climb rate is limited to that of the tow-plane, so a launch takes longer

You will be introduced to the aerotow launch in the same back to front fashion as you are to winching and auto-towing, but it is described here in its 'real' order.

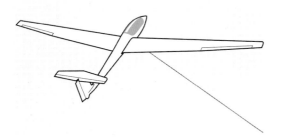

In the full climb.

tow cable strongly enough and at more than a certain angle, it can lift up the back end of the tow-car sufficiently for the drive wheels to lose traction.

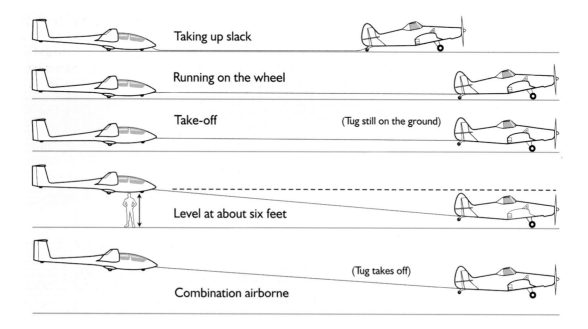

Taking up slack

Running on the wheel

Take-off (Tug still on the ground)

Level at about six feet

Combination airborne (Tug takes off)

Aerotow take-off.

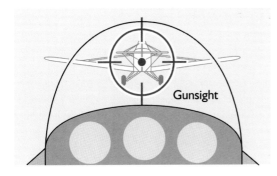

Maintaining station on aerotow.

Once the glider has left the ground do NOT allow it to climb away, winch-launch fashion, as you will very quickly tip the tug onto its nose and do for the pilot. Allow the glider to rise to about 6ft above the ground, and then hold it there, following the tug.

One way to keep station once the combination is airborne is to imagine that you are trying to shoot the tug down. Keep the tug in an imaginary gunsight. If the tug goes up or down, follow it, but without making sudden or large elevator movements. It isn't always necessary to do something to follow the tug. Generally, if the tug moves up or down in relation to you without changing its attitude, it has flown into rising or sinking air. You will pass through this a few seconds later and rise or sink as well, which will put you back where you were before the tug changed its position.

When the tug turns, bank by the same amount and follow it round. Don't try to move into a position where you are looking directly at the back of the tug as that will put you outside its circle – see the illustration below. You will find it difficult to stay there because the circle you are following is larger than the tug's, so even though you won't catch it up you will be going faster; and you are much more likely to get too high and then either start overtaking the tug or tip it up. The correct view of the tug during a turn should be from a position that will appear to be slightly inside the turn.

There will be a number of exercises to do on tow, such as returning from positions off to one side, or slightly too high or low. In the later stages you will be asked to fly the glider round the tug's slipstream – known as 'boxing the slipstream' – which takes you through the low tow position (see diagram on next page). In this country a low tow is normally reserved for aerotow retrieves where there can be long periods of level flight. If low towing you must return to the normal tow position above the slipstream before releasing, to avoid being hit by the rings on your end of the rope.

Release

Before release have a good look round, both to see if there is any other traffic about and to check where the glider is in relation to the airfield. When happy that all is clear and the airfield is within easy reach, check that the rope has some tension in it and then pull the release. If the rope isn't

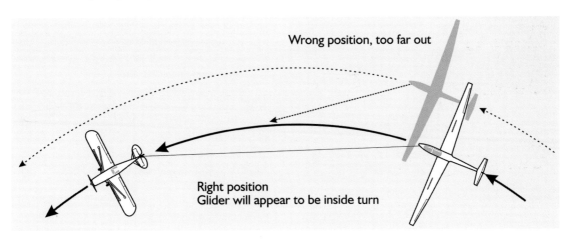

Following the tug in turns.

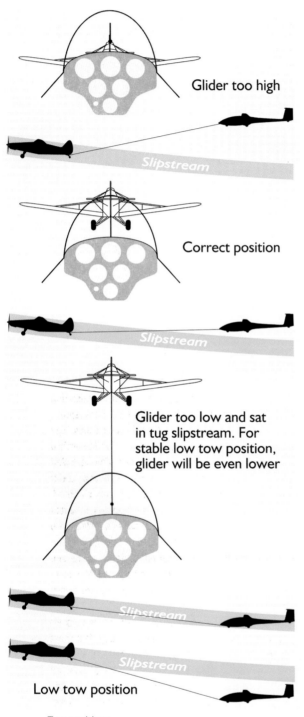

Glider too high

Correct position

Glider too low and sat in tug slipstream. For stable low tow position, glider will be even lower

Low tow position

Tow positions.

under some slight tension the tug pilot may not know you've released. When the rope has gone – it usually snakes away ahead – pull up into a gentle climbing turn to the left. The tug will dive away to the right. At some clubs gliders go to the right after release, and tugs to the left. Whichever way you turn, or even if you just go straight ahead, you must also go up somewhat to avoid hitting the rope or rings.

EMERGENCY PROCEDURES

It is essential that you react appropriately to rope or cable breaks. Because of the angle of climb winch/auto-tow failures are potentially more serious for the glider pilot than aerotow rope breaks or tug failures, and the procedures differ.

Cable breaks and winch failures

You can save yourself a great deal of potential trouble when winching by never being in a steep nose up attitude and slow or low at the same time. The glider will only fly if the airspeed is adequate, but if the cable breaks when the glider is climbing, the 'gravity engine' (discussed earlier) immediately starts to act backwards as a brake. The steeper the climb the swifter the deceleration and loss of airspeed. The first thing to do is lower the nose quickly to well below the normal flying attitude. This allows the speed to build up rapidly to at least the approach speed you decided on during the Eventualities part of the pre-take-off checks! Put the speed on first, and don't turn – if that's what you've decided you must do – until you have it. Only then pull the release to drop any lengths of cable which may still be dangling from the hook.

There are occasions when the technique just described needs modifying. For example, if the break occurs just after you've taken off and are in a shallow climb, then pushing hard forward on the stick will dive you into the ground. Likewise, if you react to the weak link breaking when the launch is fast, then you could end up flying the glider underneath the cable and its parachute, which can cause problems. While the broad admonition to 'lower the nose' is correct, the exact circumstances may require modification either to how much you do so, or how quickly you do it.

A genuine break is usually very sudden and there's no mistaking what has happened. There is usually a

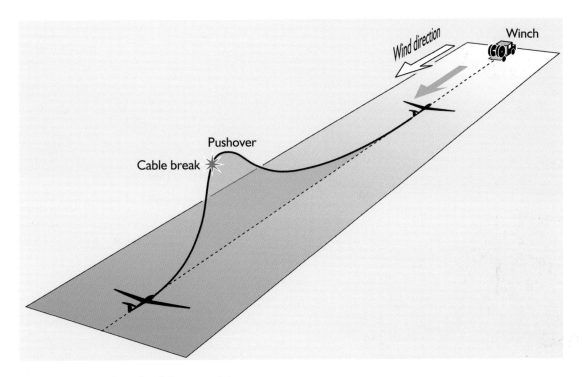

Cable break and landing ahead. If you can, do!

loud clunk and the glider immediately starts to decelerate. The situation that can catch you out if you aren't on the ball is the incremental failure where, say, the winch engine gradually packs up, or you have a low break when the climb attitude is shallow and there is no great tension in the cable. These two types of failure don't necessarily advertize themselves with any noise, and any deceleration may be quite slow. If you aren't monitoring the ASI you may not notice what's happening. In either case, you need to respond quickly, but as before, what you do will depend on (a) the attitude and speed of the glider at the time of the break and (b) your height.

As to where to land, the general rule is to land ahead if you can safely do so. However, if you have a break at, let's say, 400ft and only lower the nose to the normal flying attitude rather than what's actually needed, then most of the airfield ahead will be hidden under the nose (see diagram on page 96). Your first thought will be 'not enough room' and you will decide to turn. At this point a little bell should go off in your head. Remember the earlier demon-

stration of spinning off a cable break? Lower the nose first to below the normal flying attitude! If there is any appreciable wind down the run you will be surprised how high you can be and still land straight ahead inside the airfield boundary. You will need to have this demonstrated because airbrake effectiveness varies between glider types, and the length of gliding fields is hardly standard. Some are quite small, so local terrain and other factors may require slightly different techniques, even though the basic decisions still remain the same. Depending on the height at which the break occurred, various options are open to you which will vary from landing straight ahead, as described, to a complete circuit (see diagram above and on page 105).

Very low breaks are a special case, as mentioned earlier (see diagram on pages 104 and 105). The most important point is not to react blindly. If you're very close to the ground, provided the glider is more or less level, all that may be required is to hold the attitude and let the glider sink back onto the ground. Don't use the airbrakes. You're not going to go fly off the end of the airfield.

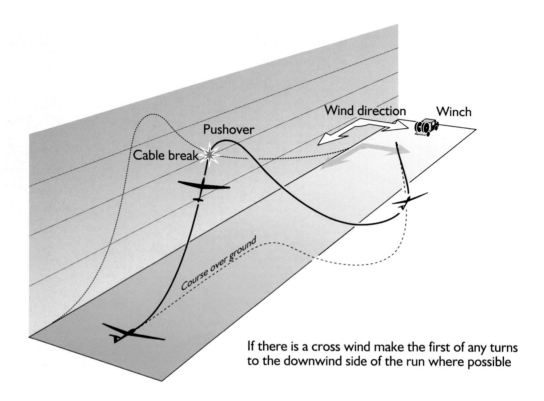

Wind direction   Winch

Pushover

Cable break

Course over ground

If there is a cross wind make the first of any turns
to the downwind side of the run where possible

Cable break and 'S' turn. 'S' turns are discouraged, but are sometimes the only available option.

AEROTOW ROPE BREAKS & TUG FAILURES

The signals from the tug

On tow the tug waggles its rudder coarsely

This signal is the tug pilot telling you that the glider's airbrakes are out. Regardless of how they managed to come out in the first place, check the position of the airbrake lever and glance at the wing to see if they really are out or not. Close them!

The tug rocks its wings

This signal means 'release immediately', but there's no point in pulling the release and creating an emergency where there was none before. Don't confuse gust induced rocking of the wings with that caused by the pilot. Watch the tug's ailerons. When the ailerons move first and the tug then banks positively first one way and then the other, it's a signal. If the tug is in serious trouble you may be jettisoned without any warning. You can glide a great deal further without an engine than the tow-plane can, so ditch the rope and decide what to do. If you did the Eventualities part of the pre-flight check correctly, you will have an appropriate strategy already in mind.

Glider unable to release from tow

This 'hang-up' is exceedingly rare and you are far more likely to have a rope break or an inadvertent release. There is no back-release on a nose aerotow hook, so if you can't let go of the rope, fly the glider well out to the tug's left and rock your wings; left wing down first so that you don't instantly slide back behind the tug. A small amount of airbrake might be needed to prevent a big bow developing in the rope. Landings on tow are possible but the tug pilot may just tow you back to the airfield and release you there.

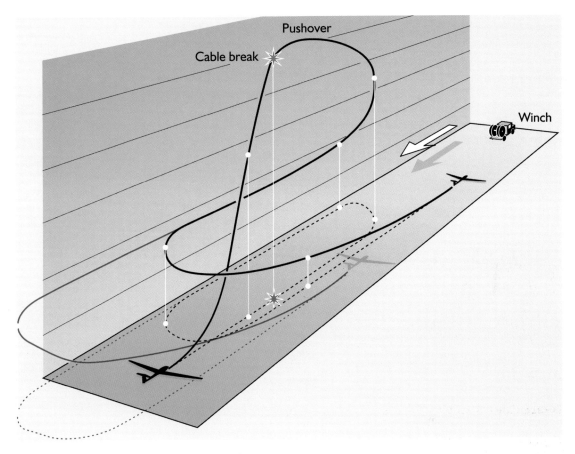

Cable break at a height which allows a truncated circuit.

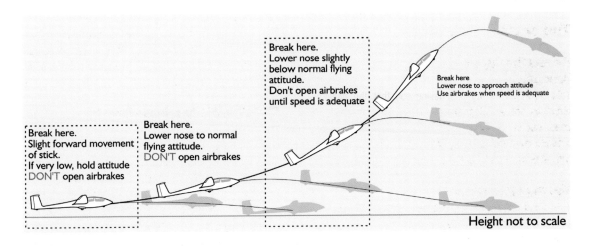

Very low cable breaks.

You now have about 180ft of strong rope streaming back underneath the glider. Don't come in low over the boundary hedge as the rope could easily snag, with possibly disastrous results. Land well into the airfield.

If any of these emergencies happen for real during your training the likelihood is that the instructor will take over. But one day you will be solo and you must know the signals and act accordingly.

THE CIRCUIT

Circuit planning

A flight can be divided into three blocks, two of which are more or less fixed in duration. Block one is the launch, and block three is the circuit. Individually, both last about the same length of time every flight. Block two is the rest of the flight – duration elastic. We've already looked at block one, the launch. Now for the other fixed bit, block three.

Imagine a situation where you winch launch to 1,000ft in absolutely still air. Were the glider to continue on in a straight line after release it would travel, at best, a certain

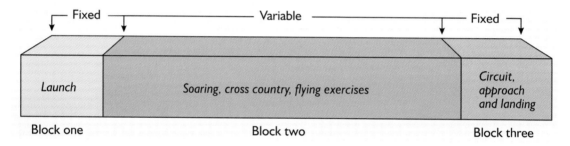

Phases of flight.

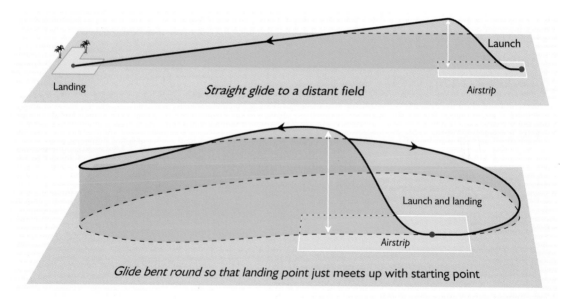

Evolution of the circuit.

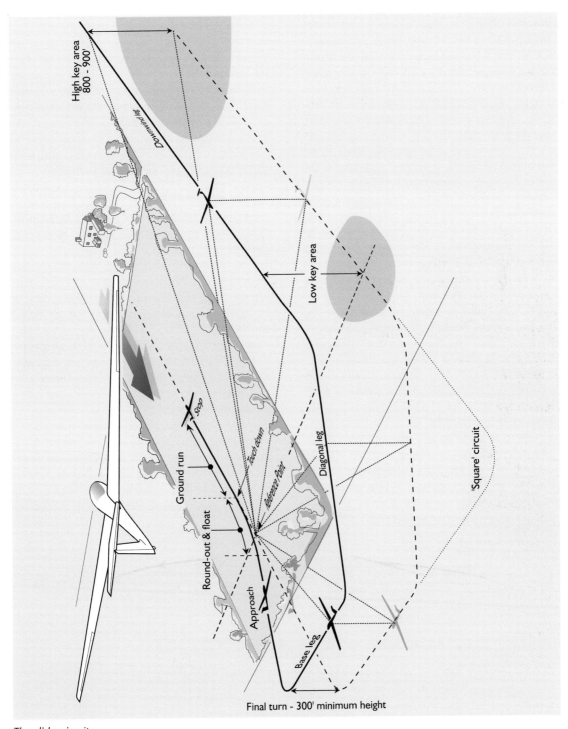

The glider circuit.

maximum distance before touching down, 7.6 miles if the best glide ratio was 40:1. For convenience, if nothing else, it makes sense to bend what would otherwise be a straight glide to a distant field in such a way that you just manage to arrive back where you started. Given that the air is never completely still and that human judgement is far from perfect, such a 'just-make-it-back' technique would result eventually in the glider failing to make the airfield, and quite likely burying itself in the downwind hedge. At the other extreme, arriving back too high would lead to the glider over-shooting and going through the upwind hedge.

Anyone can hit the ground any time, anywhere, but a good landing at the position of your choice is what counts, and the circuit is the necessary preparation for this. In ideal circumstances the circuit (block three) begins in the 'high key' area at about 700–800ft, upwind and to one side of the proposed landing area. The high key area is, as it says, an area and not a point, so the circuit does not have to start always in exactly the same place. The downwind leg runs parallel to the proposed direction of landing and not too close to it, though this will depend a bit on the height available. The low key area is opposite the Reference Point (RP, discussed later). Powered aircraft do square circuits, but gliders chop off a corner to keep the RP in view at all times, starting a diagonal leg (45 degrees to the downwind leg) just before the RP disappears behind the wing. The base leg is at right angles to the approach path and may be quite short. The final turn should be at no less than 300ft, but sufficiently close to the landing area for the glider to be able to reach the airfield easily – see later note on the approach.

Demonstration circuits will have shown you what looks right and what doesn't, and how to judge the correct angles, distances and heights in relation to the RP, which will be somewhat short of where the glider will actually touch down. During the circuit you need to keep a constant check on the whereabouts of other traffic, and while monitoring your progress don't forget to note whether the landing area remains clear or not.

APPROACH, ROUND-OUT AND LANDING

Landing can be one of the trickier aspects of flight, and the requirement to be so close to the ground to do it doesn't help. Ideally the approach and landing should as near as possible straight into wind. Landing downwind has two major drawbacks. First, the approach angle for any given airbrake setting and airspeed will be shallower than the equivalent approach into wind, and second, the ground speed will be higher than the airspeed. At this stage of the flight that's completely the wrong way round because the controls rely on airspeed to function, and with a tail wind they will stop working long before the glider has stopped moving during the ground run.

The approach needs to start at the right place, as described later, towards a suitable landing area, and at a steady speed which will usually be higher than the normal flying speed – but see approach speeds below. The round-out needs to begin at the right height and the 'float', which is the part of the landing sequence where the glider starts to slow in preparation for touch-down, is, in effect, an

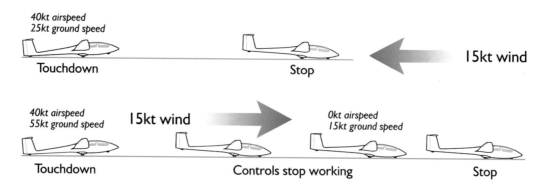

Why land into wind?

exercise in preventing the glider from landing. As for the actual touch-down itself, if that is made correctly and at the right speed there will be no chance of the glider taking off again. The ground run is the reverse of the take-off run and largely a matter of keeping the wings level and the glider running straight until it stops.

Approach speeds and the wind gradient

On a day where there is little or no wind the minimum approach speed should be about 15kt above the glider's stalling speed. Use of the airbrakes can significantly increase the stalling speed in some gliders, so that also has to be taken into account. If the wind is moderate to strong, or conditions are at all gusty, the rule of thumb is to add 5kt to the minimum approach speed for every 10kt increase in wind speed. The reason for making the increase is because the wind speed increases with height (a 'wind gradient'), and the biggest changes tend to occur within the first few hundred feet of the ground. If the approach is begun at too low a speed for the conditions (see illustration below), the glider can lose vital airspeed as it descends through the

gradient, and then have insufficient height remaining in which to accelerate and make up the difference. In the worst case this means an 'arrival' in a fully stalled condition. In any event, if conditions are rough and/or windy, the chosen approach speed (Eventualities!) should make due allowance for these things.

Use of the airbrakes

If there were no means of controlling both the speed and steepness of the approach, landing where you wanted would be difficult, particularly in a modern glider. Long shallow approaches are very unsafe because the glide performance will probably be near its best and the only available adjustment is to make it worse. If you are already undershooting you can only undershoot even more! Making a steeper approach without any airbrakes would simply lead to the glider gaining extra speed, and then being very reluctant to land until you were well up the airfield, if not actually off the end.

The primary purpose of the glider's airbrakes is to create extra drag. The most important results of this are to steepen the glide angle (effectively to worsen the performance) and

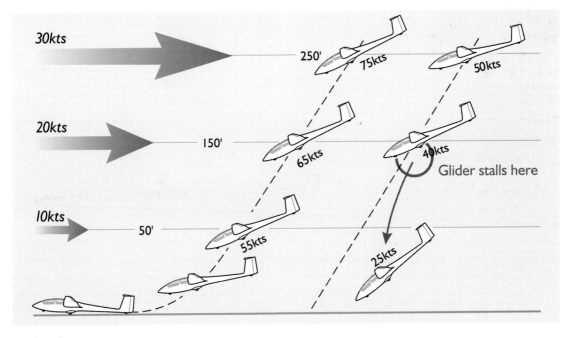

Wind gradient.

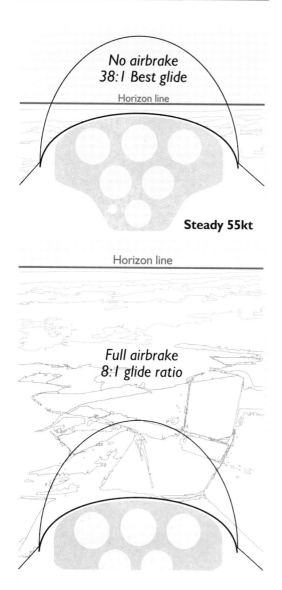

Attitude with airbrakes, airspeed constant.

increase the rate of descent. Additionally, if you maintain a constant attitude when opening the airbrakes, the extra drag will cause you to slow down. So, in practice, if you open the airbrakes to increase the rate of descent, then you may have to lower the nose to maintain the speed. Likewise, if you close the airbrakes to decrease the descent rate, you may need to raise the nose slightly to prevent the glider accelerating. Be warned that opening the brakes can

change the attitude of the glider without you doing anything else. Some gliders pitch down, others pitch up. Briefings will emphasize that it is the airbrakes that control the rate of descent and the elevator which controls the speed.

Also worth remembering are that the more airbrake you use the longer the glider will take to accelerate to a given speed – so always set the correct approach speed before you open them. A further point is that the moment you unlock the airbrakes of some gliders they will try and open fully, so watch out for that.

The approach cone

The final turn needs to be at about 300ft (preferably no lower, and higher if the wind is strong) and just far enough down-wind of the landing area that if you maintain a steady speed and use half to two thirds airbrake you will still get there. As you turn onto the approach there will stretch ahead of you an invisible cone whose lower edge is the glide path with full airbrake, and top edge the glide path with no airbrake. The optimum (ie the most adjustable) approach path uses half to two thirds airbrake – which takes the glider more or less straight down the middle of the cone (see diagram on next page and note how the wind affects the cone's shape). Your RP (see below) should lie at the end of the optimum approach path, but it can only be there if you begin the approach from the right position. There is plenty of leeway here but judging where the approach needs to begin can take a bit of practice.

If, when you make the final turn you find yourself slightly too far back to use the optimum approach path, leave the airbrakes shut and fly forward until you have intercepted the correct line.

Using the reference point (RP)

As described, the circuit is planned in relation to the RP, and when you have turned onto the approach you use the RP to judge whether you are over-shooting or under-shooting. The idea is to keep the speed steady on the approach and the RP ahead of you, in the same place on the canopy. If you come down the approach and the RP moves towards you and looks set to slide underneath (it will have to at some point, when you start to round-out), then you are over–shooting. Open the airbrakes slightly and adjust the attitude to

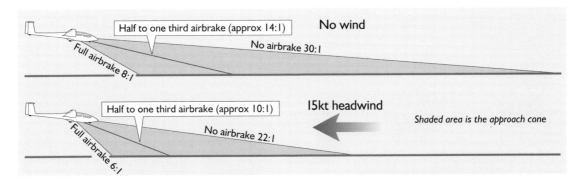

The approach cone.

maintain the speed. If the RP moves up the canopy, you are under–shooting. You may need to close the airbrakes slightly and raise the nose a small amount to maintain your selected approach speed (see diagram opposite).

Once you are established on the approach and are definitely going to reach the RP, freeze the airbrakes and try to avoid fiddling about with them unless the speed is dropping off, particularly during the round-out. If you do start popping the airbrakes in or out at this point you will either hit the ground rather hard, balloon upwards, or wobble away down the airfield for a considerable distance before you touch down again.

Keeping the speed steady is very important because if you don't you can easily keep the RP in the same position on the canopy, and still over- or under-shoot. In an instance of over-shooting, you have chosen an RP that's far too near to you for the height you have. Naturally, when it starts to move towards you, you lower the nose to keep it in the 'correct' place. The speed will build and by the time you've rounded out there will be a lot of it to get rid of before touch-down. As shown in the illustration on the next page, the opposite happens if the approach began too low, or too far away (they amount to the same thing). To keep the RP in the same position in this case you will be gradually raising the nose and slowing down, and may well drop heavily short of your intended touch down point.

Landing: round-out, float and touchdown

It is easy to become fixated on the RP, but it is an aid to circuit planning and approach control only, and at some point you will

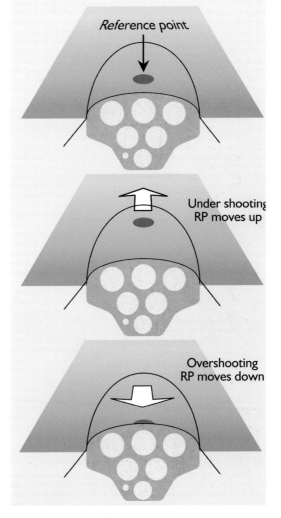

Movement of the Reference Point (RP).

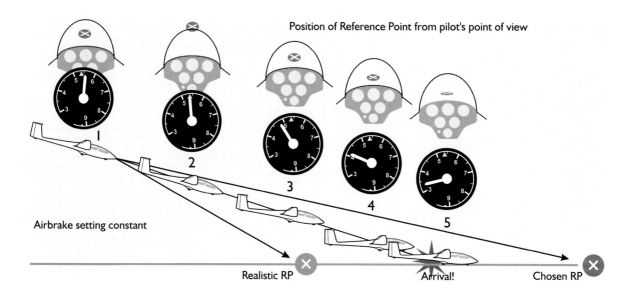

Position of Reference Point from pilot's point of view

Airbrake setting constant

Realistic RP

Arrival!

Chosen RP

One result of failing to keep the approach speed steady and using the RP as an aiming point (which it is not).

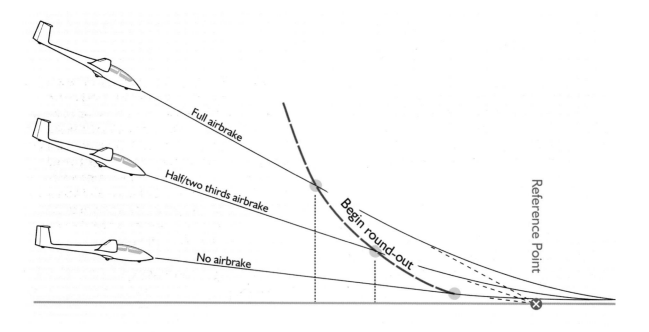

Full airbrake

Half/two thirds airbrake

No airbrake

Begin round-out

Reference Point

Round-out point.

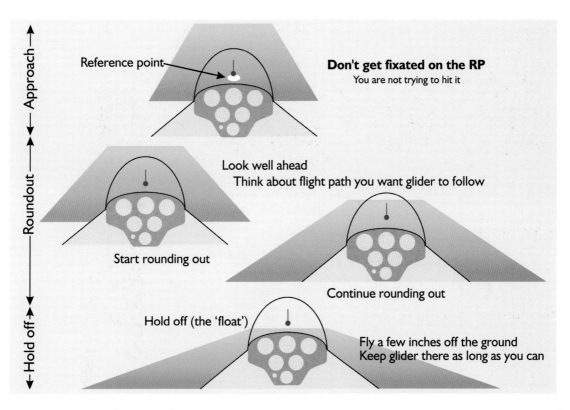

Approach
Roundout
Hold off

Reference point

Don't get fixated on the RP
You are not trying to hit it

Look well ahead
Think about flight path you want glider to follow

Start rounding out

Continue rounding out

Hold off (the 'float')

Fly a few inches off the ground
Keep glider there as long as you can

Changing perspective during round-out.

have to start rounding-out (bringing the nose up) if you don't want to do an expensive imitation of a dart into a dartboard. What you are aiming for is that by the time the glider reaches the ground it will be flying level a few inches up, and there you will hold it until it touches down of its own accord. You will have been asked to follow through on the controls during previous landings done by your instructor, so you will have some idea of where the round-out ought to start. In general, the steeper the approach the sooner the round-out needs to begin.

What won't be so obvious is when to stop using the RP (you are not trying to hit it) and look much further ahead. Looking ahead helps you to judge the rate of descent more accurately (by the time you're level it needs to be zero!), and the changing perspectives and general texture of the ground will give useful clues as to your height.

Begin the round-out at a height that isn't so low that it involves a sudden and sharp change in attitude, nor so high that the glider starts to slow down well before it is 'in the float' or 'hold-off' (where the glider is flying level a few inches

off the ground). Once the glider is in the hold-off, keep it there. Don't let it land. As it slows down it will start to sink. Use a gentle and gradually increasing back pressure on the stick to keep the glider just airborne until it is in the landing attitude (see illustration on p98, and overleaf), and then hold it in that. If you have everything just right and don't play around with the airbrakes the glider will touch down smoothly of its own accord, main and tail wheel together. The flight has not ended until the glider stops, so don't relax as soon as you make contact with the ground. Savour the moment of triumph by all means, but keep the glider under control.

CIRCUITS: FURTHER EXERCISES

Circuits without altimeter

Once you've grasped the basic principles of circuit planning, you will then do circuits without using the altimeter. For your

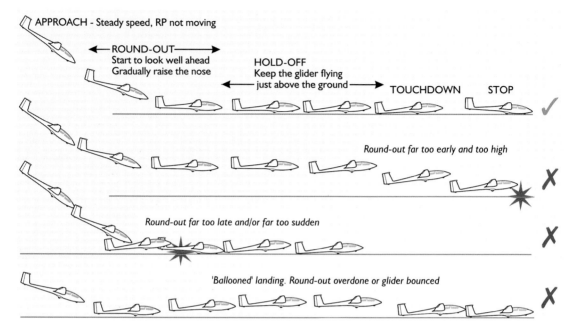

APPROACH - Steady speed, RP not moving

←——ROUND-OUT——→
Start to look well ahead
Gradually raise the nose

HOLD-OFF
Keep the glider flying
←—— just above the ground ——→ TOUCHDOWN   STOP ✓

Round-out far too early and too high ✗

Round-out far too late and/or far too sudden ✗

'Ballooned' landing. Round-out overdone or glider bounced ✗

Rounding-out – correct and incorrect ways of doing it.

first field landing, and indeed any subsequent field landings, the altimeter will be, at best, inaccurate – due to changes in air pressure or differences in height between the field and where you took off – and, at worst, totally misleading. Circuits without it are much easier than one might think.

For the exercise the altimeter is either covered over before take-off, or the instructor will ask you to wind it to some silly setting once you've released from the launch. The decision when and from where to start the circuit, and the location of the key points, is left entirely to you. If you have been using the altimeter too much, or using secondary RPs, this exercise will show up your bad habits. Secondary RPs, as opposed to the RP, are objects on and around the airfield which you may be using, probably unconsciously, to plan the circuit. For example, the clump of trees by the small pond on the boundary may be where you always turn onto the diagonal leg at 400ft indicated, or perhaps you always follow a road for the downwind leg. If you are using such landmarks to 'plot' your way towards touchdown somewhere 'over there' – i.e., you are treating them like navigational waypoints – then you will be in trouble if you have to land somewhere else, where the landmarks won't be the same.

The circuit without altimeter is an excellent test of your judgement. In order for it to have its full effect you may be asked to land in an out-of-the-way corner of the airfield from a circuit whose legs don't lie parallel or at right angles to anything. Again, the circuit must be planned in relation to where you want to touch down.

Approaches from awkward positions

Sooner or later you will inadvertently engineer one of these for yourself, reaching the airfield at the wrong height and in the wrong position for a normal circuit. It is best to know what to do because an off-field landing (outlanding) can be regarded also as an approach from an awkward position. For the exercise the instructor will take control and fly the glider to some point over or near the airfield from which a normal circuit is either impossible or a very poor choice, but usually not so far away that you can't land on the airfield, somewhere. Then control will be handed over to you. Size up the situation if you haven't done so already. The first priority is to land safely and preferably more or less into wind – it doesn't matter

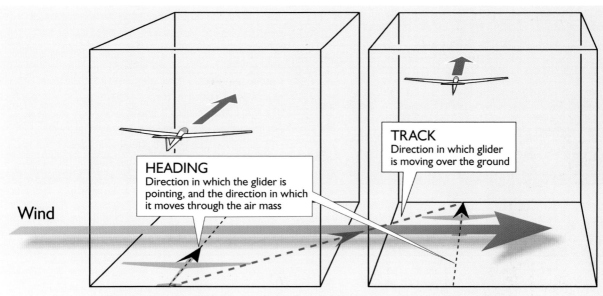

HEADING
Direction in which the glider is pointing, and the direction in which it moves through the air mass

TRACK
Direction in which glider is moving over the ground

Wind

Glider flies through the air mass as the air mass moves over the ground

Air mass and glider movement – drift.

where. Land on the airfield if you can, but don't try and get back to the launch point through some misconceived notion of saving either yourself or everyone else any hassle. Do what is safe, not what appears to be convenient for everyone else.

Circuits in high winds

The main differences from previous circuits in moderate or no wind will be the height and position of the final turn, and the approach speed. The gradient effects mentioned earlier are very significant in strong winds, and if you are landing in windy conditions at a hill top site, 20kt plus of airspeed can easily disappear within a hundred feet of descent. For such conditions the final turn will be made higher than usual, and the approach speed must be faster to take into account the effects of the wind gradient. The gradient effects work in reverse if you are taking off, ie you will gain speed as you go up through it. It is worth thinking about the effect this might have on a winch cable break at low altitude.

CROSSWIND TAKE-OFFS AND LANDINGS

General points

Think of still air as being a large block on the ground. A glider flies through this block in a straight line, at 50kt and in balanced flight. In whichever direction the glider is 'heading', its 'track' over the ground is the same. When the wind blows, the block through which the glider is flying moves over the ground, and unless the glider happens to be going directly into wind, or directly downwind, its heading and track will differ. The difference between the two is known as the 'drift angle', or simply as 'drift'.

When heading directly up or down wind at a constant indicated airspeed, the only obvious changes are to your ground speed. If the glider flies directly into a 20kt wind at an airspeed of 50kt it will have a ground speed of 50 – 20kt, or 30kt. For every 50 units the glider travels forward it is carried back by 20. With the same airspeed and a 20kt tailwind the ground speed will be 50+20kt, or 70kt; for every 50 units the glider travels forwards it is carried a further 20. For the same indicated airspeed there is a 40kt

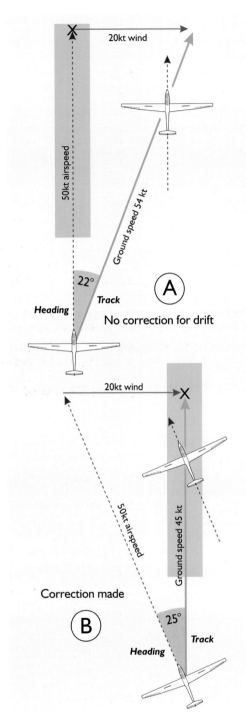

Drift and corrections.

difference in the ground speeds. If you mistake ground speed for airspeed – and it is not difficult to do – you may, in the case of a tail wind, think that you are flying too fast and attempt to slow down. This can lead to unsafe situations, particularly if you are in the circuit and about to turn. When it comes to staying airborne and in control, airspeed is what counts, not ground speed, so if you are in any doubt about how fast you are going, refer to the ASI.

Example A (illustration opposite) shows a glider flying at 50kt with a 20kt 90 degree crosswind from the left. In this case, for every 50 units the glider moves forwards the airmass moves it 20 units to the right. You can draw this all out on a piece of paper and measure the results. The glider tracks off about 22 degrees to the right of the heading, and has a ground speed (not an airspeed) of about 54kt.

Example B shows a glider flying a heading at 50kt airspeed that allows it to track, in this case, straight up the page. Note that the new heading is 25 degrees left of the track, and that the glider's ground speed is 45kts.

Crosswind landings

Much of the training is aimed at getting you to fly accurately, without slip or skid, so the visual cues presented by drift can and do cause some confusion. Take the example of a crosswind landing: let's say the wind is again 20kt and from the left, at right angles to the landing run. If you simply line up the glider parallel to the run it will drift off sideways to the right and very likely miss the run altogether. For the approach path to be directly down the run the glider must head into wind by an amount related to the crosswind component and the glider's airspeed. The visual paradox that tends to throw most people is that when the appropriate 'laying off' into wind is made, the glider appears to be flying sideways even though the string is slap bang in the middle.

Treat the whole exercise exactly like a normal landing, a bit skew perhaps, and keep in balanced flight down the approach. Taking the crosswind to be 90 degrees from the left, just as you are about to touch down the ground will be coming at you from the right hand side, so you must use right rudder to yaw the glider to line up with it – this is called 'kicking off the drift'. If there is a lot of drift you will need a lot of rudder, and perhaps a small amount of opposite aileron to prevent the glider banking. 'Kick off' at the right moment and the glider will land without any drift. Kick off too early and you will have do it again a bit later, having already swung yourself either more crosswind or even slightly downwind in the process. If you kick off too late the glider will touch down sideways, which is both uncomfortable and can cause damage. If the crosswind component is very strong the glider will almost certainly weathercock into wind towards the end of the ground run, and you won't be able to stop it doing so.

Try and allow for all the foregoing when deciding how near or far away to land from other gliders on the ground. If you swing on landing it may be towards the launch point and any parked gliders/cars, people etc.

Crosswind take-off

The chief problem with a crosswind take-off is that during the first part of the ground run, when the controls aren't very effective, the glider will try to weathercock into wind. At the same time, the into-wind wing may try to lift up and bank the glider out of wind. The slower the initial acceleration the more pronounced these effects will be, so crosswind aerotow take-offs tend to be far more difficult to handle than winch launches. A lot can depend also on the type of glider you're flying.

Don't wait until a swing develops before you do something about it because if the crosswind is strong you will be too late! Begin the ground run with out-of-wind rudder already applied – the degree depending on the strength of the crosswind component. If the upwind wing is likely to lift, apply a small amount of into-wind aileron before the glider starts moving, and be ready to adjust the rudder and aileron quickly, as necessary.

If the glider has an offset winch hook then a crosswind from one side can present problems with swing, whereas a crosswind of the same strength from the other side may have little or no effect. Under rapid acceleration the effect of an offset hook will be much greater than with a slower acceleration.

During a crosswind aerotow the glider will take off first and then immediately start to drift sideways. If allowed to do so it can become so far out of line that the tug can't keep straight and is swung round into wind, which may cause it to run off the strip (see diagram on page 119). To avoid this, once the glider is airborne, turn it 'into wind' sufficiently to maintain position directly behind the tug, and tracking parallel to the run. Watch the bank angle when you do this because

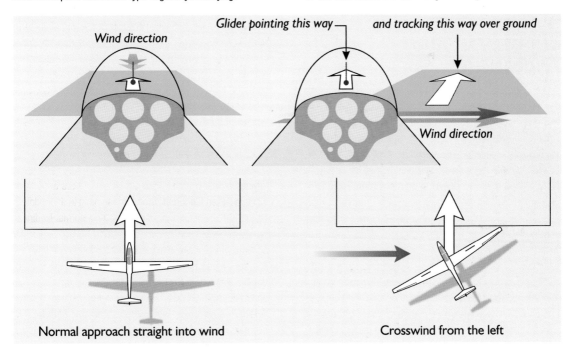

Cross-wind landing.

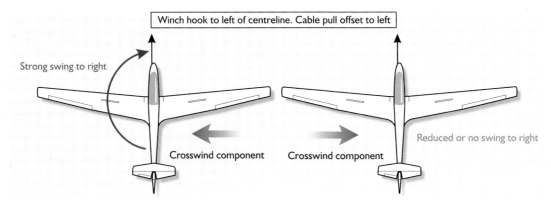

Winch hook to left of centreline. Cable pull offset to left

Strong swing to right

Crosswind component

Crosswind component

Reduced or no swing to right

Offset launch hooks and crosswind take-off.

you won't be very high at the time. Once the tug has left the ground the entire combination will drift with the wind and the glider will need to be brought back into line with the tug.

Depending on the club site and the number of runs it has, you may get lots of practice at crosswind take-off and landing, or none worth speaking of. Try and get some because you will have to operate with a crosswind at some time or another, possibly at another site or during a field landing, so it is best to be familiar with the technique.

JUDGEMENT AND AIRMANSHIP

Perhaps the best way to describe judgement is to say that it is the pilot's appreciation of what is realistically possible in a given set of circumstances. At a more mundane level, something like circuit judgement requires placing the various key points where they are appropriate for the height available. So it would be good judgement to turn in early to land if you were low in the circuit, and very poor judgement to keep trudging on round the 'normal' circuit pattern if you were several hundred feet lower than was usually the case.

It is good judgement not to push things so far that you have only one not very attractive option left open to you, particularly if that happens to be a crash! Obviously, as you get closer to the ground, your cone of options, as it were, is narrowing to the single point of landing. There are only so many courses of action open to a pilot in a given situation, but it is best to have as many rather than as few as possible available.

Airmanship is difficult to describe because so many different factors are involved. If you go hell for leather into a thermal, zoom up into a stupendous climb and then wrap yourself around the core of the thermal without much thought beyond your own satisfaction, everyone nearby will be scattering for their lives. Your airmanship will have been poor – deplorable, in fact. Airmanship is, in one respect, a matter of looking after other pilots' safety as well as your own. For example, you might stay on aerotow a bit longer than intended so that when the tug pilot dives away after release, he or she will be in no danger of hitting the other glider that you have seen just below and to your right. This isn't an assumption on your part that the tug pilot is blind – they won't be any more in favour of a mid-air collision than you – but, like gliders, tugs also have their blind spots. Whatever the exact definition of airmanship, it is largely about aerial awareness and consideration for others, and much of it comes with training and experience.

GOING SOLO

The frequently asked question 'how long will it take me to go solo?' is a 'how long is a piece of string?' question, because the answer will be based on your aptitude, the amount of free time you have, and on how well you are taught. People have gone solo after 35 flights, and a few have taken as long as 150. A tiny number never go solo, but there is no reason why you should be one of those. The average number of winch launches to solo is about 50, whereas although the average number of aerotows to solo will be somewhat lower, the flight times will be longer.

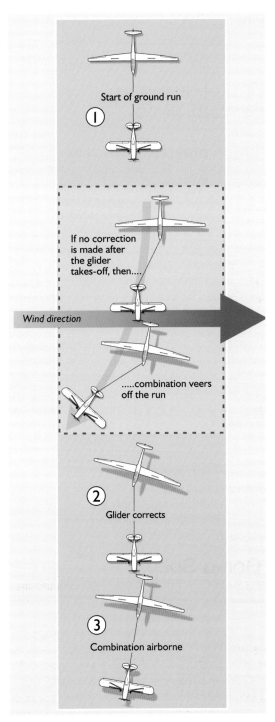

Start of ground run

①

If no correction
is made after
the glider
takes-off, then....

Wind direction

.....combination veers
off the run

②

Glider corrects

③

Combination airborne

Aerotow and cross-winds.

Going solo is one of the great experiences in gliding. Once your instructors are happy that you know the basics, are consistent in your responses, and can not only make good decisions but make sensible changes if need be ('not losing the plot' is the phrase), they will sign your logbook to say that you are 'OK for solo'. Then it's off on your own. People vary quite a bit in their reactions to this moment, but it is definitely one of the big milestones that you will never forget, even if your reaction at the time is a bit muted. A few people are a bit surprised that it failed to be more dramatic. Most instructors are glad that it wasn't!

It is common practice these days to send you off solo in the glider on which you've been trained or, in the case of a club which has several different types of two-seater, the one which you've been flying on the day. Everything should be familiar to you, but a nice surprise is that the glider may handle better and be somewhat lighter on the controls than it was with two of you aboard.

Do you need or get a licence?

The BGA will issue you with a tiny booklet which counts as a licence and requires a passport photograph. The booklet has space for the badge flights that you may do if you continue gliding. Strictly speaking it isn't a licence as such, nor is there currently a requirement for one. There is talk of a more formal licence for glider pilots, and the situation may change further under the auspices of EASA and European 'harmonization'. Whatever happens, the paperwork won't get any less.

Keeping in practice

Once solo it definitely pays to keep in practice. Most clubs will require you to take annual check flights and to fly often enough during the year to stay current. The requirements for currency vary from club to club – often dependent on the kind of glider fleet they have – but they are not impossibly high and should be regarded as the bare minimum. Flying requires judgement and motor skills, and it is judgement that tends to deteriorate if the skills involved aren't sufficiently exercised. That's not to say that you will be hugely at risk if you don't fly at least once a month, for example, or do less than a certain number of hours. However, there is an 'edge' to all forms of aviation – as

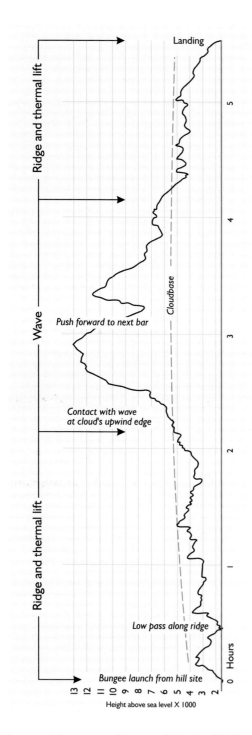

Barograph/logger trace (annotated after the flight).

there probably is to any worthwhile sport – and it marks out the subtle but significant difference between being in and with an aeroplane, and being sat uneasily on top of it.

PROGRESSING BEYOND SOLO

How to progress after solo
After solo there can be a period where you find yourself wondering 'what next?'. Having reached the great goal of solo for which you struggled so mightily, what else can you possibly do that's even half as exciting? To encourage you to progress and give you goals if you want them, there are badges which lead you into cross country flying. You may be perfectly happy flying locally around your home airfield, and if so, don't feel that you ought to be doing something else. The badge requirements are shown in the table on the next page.

For all badge flights you will need the services of an Official Observer, who must sign various forms, pre-flight declarations (if relevant), and seal cameras, barographs (see the trace in illustration) or data loggers. An Official Observer is required after any badge flight to validate the results before you can send the claim to the BGA, who will otherwise reject it.

Becoming more skilful – always have some aim
Bearing in mind how easy it is to get into a rut simply because being there is the least energy-sapping option, you should make each flight count for something positive, however trivial it might seem. Gliding is relaxing, up to a point, and it can be more relaxing the more proficient you become. The crucial component, as in many other sports requiring some skill, is not to be complacent and/or lethargic. If you really are tired or upset, don't fly. If you aren't tired, then help yourself stay awake and alert by having something definite to achieve. All of the badges described opposite give you a goal for which to aim, but in order to gain those badges, particularly the later ones where the flight duration is likely to be many hours, you need to be reasonably fit, and well rested and alert before you fly.

Apres solo paper chase - description of each badge

BRONZE (specific to the UK)
1) Two flights of an hour each, or a one hour flight and one of two hours - which will count towards the cross country diploma (see below)
This badge was introduced to form a stepping stone between Solo and Silver, and to help pilots develop their soaring skills. There is a big difference between fifteen minutes in the air and the five hours plus required for a Silver.

SILVER (International badge)
The Silver badge has three parts;
1) A height gain of at least 1,000m (3,280ft) above a previous low point
2) A duration flight of at least five hours (this also gives you one leg of the Gold Badge)
3) A distance flight greater than 50km. There are a number of rules which make this slightly less than straightforward. For example, your launch height must not exceed 1% of the distance covered and you must take into account the difference in height between your take-off and landing point.

CROSS COUNTRY DIPLOMA (specific to the UK)
This was introduced by the BGA to help bridge the huge gulf between the Silver Distance (50km minimum) and the Gold (300km minimum)
Part 1: A flight round a 100km triangle (pre-declared)
Part 2: A flight round a 100km triangle (also pre-declared) at a handicapped speed of 65kph or greater.

GOLD (International badge)
1) A duration flight of at least five hours
2) A gain of height over a previous low point of at least 3,000m (9,840ft)
3) A flight to a goal at least 300km away. In practice pilots do 300km closed circuits, gaining a Diamond leg and scooping this Gold leg by default

DIAMOND (International Badge)
1) A gain of height of at least 5,000m (16,400ft). You must use supplementary oxygen for this leg.
2) A closed circuit task of at least 300km
3) A distance (to a remote land-out - quite difficult to do in the UK, but dog-legs are allowed) or a closed circuit task of at least 500km.

There are additional International Badges and Diplomas for flights of 1,000km and 2,000km

Badges.

10 Lift

KEEPING IT UP

As described earlier, gliders must always go downhill in order to maintain flying speed, so the height of the launch would seem to set the duration of any flight. In fact, for longer flights all that's required is that the air through which a glider is moving rises. If the 'up' component of the air's movement is larger than the rate at which the glider is sinking through it, then the glider will climb in relation to the ground. Imagine yourself trying to walk down an 'up' elevator. If you walk down at 2mph and the elevator is going up at 4mph, you will be carried upwards at 2mph.

There are two main causes of rising air: differences in temperature/density and obstructions. In the first category come thermals, which are usually the result of the sun heating the ground. In the second category come hill lift and wave lift, both of which are the result of something getting in the way of the wind and forcing it upwards.

When sporting gliding began, launches were either by hand or by catapult. For a flight to be anything more than a few fleet seconds, it had to begin on the top of a hill or ridge, and consisted of a straight glide down to the bottom. The gliders were then dragged back up to the top so that

Long Mynd from the south west.

Cloud streets. Wind blowing out of the picture. No wave. The thermals weren't very good, either.

122

another pilot could do the same thing. Early enthusiasts of sporting gliding must have been very fit. The oldest gliding clubs in this country tend to be situated either on the tops of ridges or close to the bottom, whereas the relative newcomers can be anywhere, quite often out in country-side which is completely flat.

Rather surprisingly, nobody either realized what was going on, or felt confident enough in the gliders and their own piloting skills to make use of the fact that when the wind blows against a hill it usually goes up and over, rather than around. Providing the vertical component of the up-slope wind is sufficiently strong, then gliders can track back and forth along the line of the hill, remaining airborne for as long as the wind decides to blow.

Once that breakthrough had been made, flight durations leapt from a matter of seconds to hours, and then days, as pilots, attempting to break records which often lasted about as long as the flights that made them, flitted up and down ridges in the dark, very often going to sleep in the process. This was a literal dead end for a few, and it wasn't long before completely avoidable accidents caused by grossly

fatigued pilots started to look a bit stupid. Even so, there were duration attempts being made as late as the 1950s, and the world record stands at about 52 hours!

HILL LIFT

A ridge or hill will only work, generally speaking if – viewed from above – the wind blows at right angles against the slope, or within a few degrees either side. If the wind hits the hill at too oblique an angle it may simply decide to skirt round it rather than rise up and over the top, or the vertical component may be unusably small. The smaller and rounder the hill, the more likely the air is to save itself the effort of upward movement and simply blow round the sides. The longer the hill the less likely this is to happen.

Using hill lift is a matter of tracking along in the band of lift created by the up-slope wind. If you are below the top of the ridge you will have to follow the contours, and the lighter the wind the closer you will need to be. Don't get too close! If you are above the ridge top, track along a line parallel to the edge of the hill and slightly forward of it. If

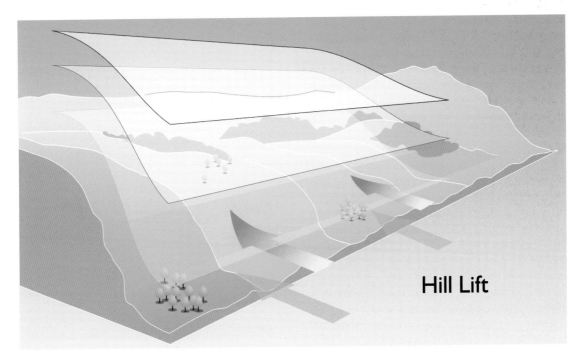

Hill Lift

Hill lift.

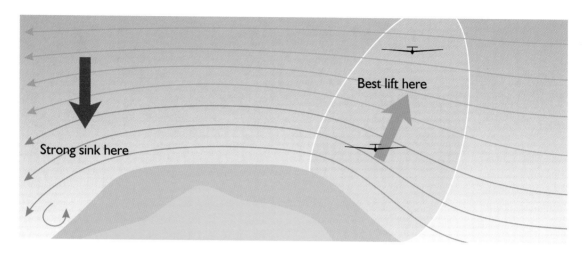

Position of best lift in relation to hill.

you go too far behind the ridge's leading edge you will experience the 'clutching hand' of the downgoing air on the lee side. This can be exceedingly strong and if you ever get caught in it you will avoid doing it again.

For obvious reasons, when you reach the end of a beat below the top, turn away from the ridge. Always increase the speed slightly before turning, as you will lose less height that way. It is also best to turn before the lift starts tailing off – better to turn in lift than sink! Up to about 600ft (local rules may set different heights), don't circle even in thermal enhanced lift because you will immediately start to drift away downwind. Even strong thermals can be squashed by the sinking air on the downwind side of a ridge, and if you haven't climbed very high by the time you arrive there it may prove impossible to return to the ridge lift against the wind. If some parts of the ridge are working markedly better than others, use figure-of-eight turns to stay there until you are high enough to do complete turns.

Remember, that in order to keep position on a ridge you have to allow for what is, in effect, a consistent and quite possibly strong crosswind, so drift is an important factor. Each beat will see the glider at an angle to the ridge, not parallel to it. One result of this is that if you are on a collision course with another glider you won't be approaching it head-on. The other glider may be easier to see, but because it is on the horizon and moving relatively slowly towards you while pointing away, the collision risk may not be obvious until fairly late on.

Landing at ridge sites that are at the top of or against the foot of a hill requires a lot more attention than landing at a flat site. Because of the clutching hand and often steep wind gradients, turbulence can also be a problem. Circuits may need to be a lot higher and closer in than they would be at a flat site. Local rules and knowledge are invaluable guides.

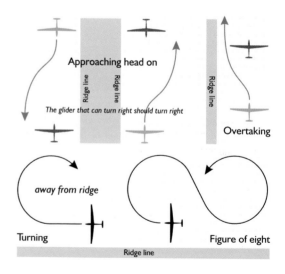

Hill soaring rules of the air.

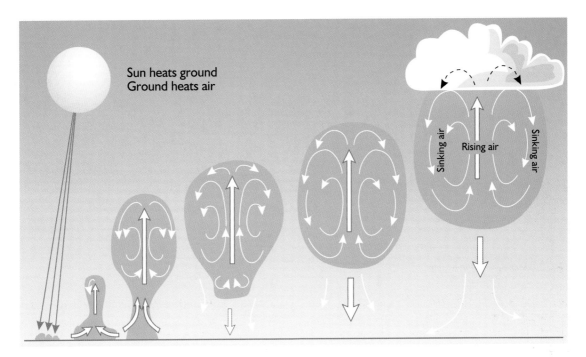

Sun heats ground
Ground heats air

Sinking air

Rising air

Sinking air

The birth and development of a thermal.

RULES OF THE AIR (RIDGES)
- Overtake other gliders on the inside, nearest the ridge
- Turns should always be away from the ridge
- When on a converging course with another glider on a ridge, the glider that can turn right, away from the ridge, should be the one to give way

THERMALS
In the 1920s glider pilots began to notice that every time a cumulus cloud passed over the ridge or hill which they were soaring, the hill lift became much stronger and could carry gliders well beyond the normal heights obtainable. When pilots who had already gone cross country by hopping from ridge to ridge explored this new form of lift, they discovered that if the sun shone, even the flattest of landscapes could provide lifting air. Hill soaring began to seem like a hamster exercising on a wheel. The emphasis changed from so called 'ridge bashing' to using the newly discovered thermals and, almost inevitably, to drifting away downwind, rather as balloons tend to do.

Thermals can form anywhere where the sun can heat the ground. The ground then heats the air directly above it (see diagram above). The ground is uneven, so the sun's heating effect is uneven, and some areas warm up more quickly than others, but once a volume of air has been warmed it becomes less dense and more buoyant than the surrounding air, and rises. As it does, cooler air is drawn in underneath and heated in turn by contact with the continually warmed ground. This process, known as convection, eventually results in huge volumes of warmed air rising into the sky like gigantic and invisible balloons.

To be able to use thermals effectively one must have some idea of what they look like, even if they are invisible. This mental model may be little more than an appreciation of the fact that thermals aren't infinite in extent, either vertically or horizontally, and that if you can fly into them you can also fly out of them just as easily. Glider pilots still argue a lot about what thermals are like and their exact shape, but apart from the intellectual challenge offered by such arguments, the main conclusion has to be that though thermals differ in their precise details, none are strong enough to disobey the laws of physics.

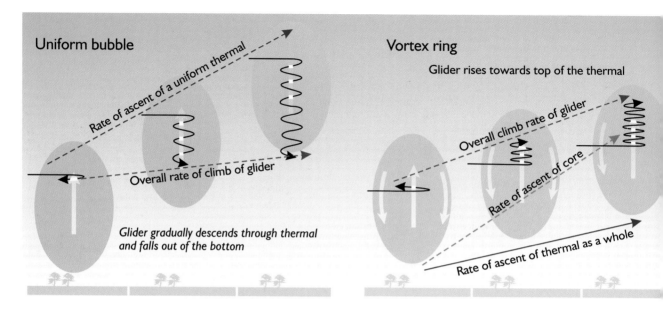

Internal flow and climb within a thermal.

Given that gliders have to run downhill continually in order to fly, it would seem that eventually they will just drop out of the bottom of any thermal, and that is what would happen if the entire thermal (the uniform bubble illustrated above) was going up at the same rate. Practical experience shows that, if anything, gliders rise towards the crown of a thermal and can remain there until the thermal dissipates, which suggests that part of the thermal rises faster than the thermal as a whole. Practical experience confirms that most thermals have a strong central core of rising air and are surrounded by a ring of sinking air. The only flow pattern that fits these facts reasonably well is a 'vortex ring', which is rather like a large smoke ring. Once this pattern of circulation has been established within a thermal 'bubble', it will continue until the thermal, gradually cooling as it rises, becomes the same temperature as the surrounding air and vanishes into small scale turbulence. The life span of a thermal is usually marked by the appearance and disappearance of cauliflower-shaped cumulus clouds, but thermals can be there even when the sky is completely cloudless, or the sun hidden behind total overcast.

THERMALLING (OR SOARING)

Finding the core

In order to achieve the highest possible climb rate the glider needs to be in the core area. Like the thermal as a whole, this is of limited diameter and the glider must circle to stay within it. One of the necessary skills, apart from being able to find the core area, is being able to keep the speed and angle of bank as constant as possible. This can be very hard work because any change in the bank angle or speed will lead to the glider describing ovals rather than circles, and eventually it will fly out of the core and possibly out of the thermal altogether.

As the glider approaches a thermal it first enters the surrounding cascade of sinking air, duly indicated by the variometer, and a short while later flies into rising air. This is also indicated on the variometer – sometimes several seconds after the glider has started to be carried upwards. This upward acceleration can be felt if the thermal core is at all strong and is a useful clue to where to go, so take notice of any such sensations. More often than not the glider will miss the core area completely, or cut obliquely through it. In the latter case there will at some point be stronger lift to one side of the glider than the other. Left to its own devices the glider would bank away from the stronger lift – A–C and A–D in the diagram on page 128. Don't allow this to happen. Turn towards the wing that is being pushed up, i.e. towards the core.

You will only be correctly centred when the variometer reading stays constant throughout the turn. If you aren't sure where the core of the thermal is, do a wide shallow turn. Tighten up when you feel the surge as you enter stronger lift, or when the in-turn wing is pushed up. If you are steeply banked and not centred, straighten up momentarily as the lift starts to increase, then return to the steep bank and see whether the situation has improved. If the thermals are small don't take all the bank off before you tighten up again. For large thermals you can roll level before turning again. It is unlikely that you will manage to centre immediately.

Thermal soaring is a skill that requires much practice, but to start with, try and fly as accurately as possible. To help you develop a good mental model of how a thermal works, use the sun or landmarks to orientate yourself. Use the trimmer also, which will help you keep the constant speed that is one ingredient of a genuinely circular circle. Always try and find the strongest lift, and turn reasonably tightly to stay with the core. If the core is both narrow and strong any increase in the glider's sink rate caused by turning tightly can be more than made up for by the stronger lift.

Streeting

It isn't always necessary to circle in thermal lift. If the wind is moderate to strong, thermals can form into long lines of lift known as 'streets', parallel to the wind direction. Streeting can vary from slightly elongated and isolated clouds to virtually continuous lines of lift, which can stretch for many miles. If the lift is in streets, so too will be the sink! Sink is usually best avoided – easy to say if you could see it – and if you are crossing from one street to another, do so at right angles to the wind since that will give you the shortest air path between them, and least time in the sinking air. If the streeting is forming at any significant angle to the wind it is usually due to the presence of wave (see page 128). For

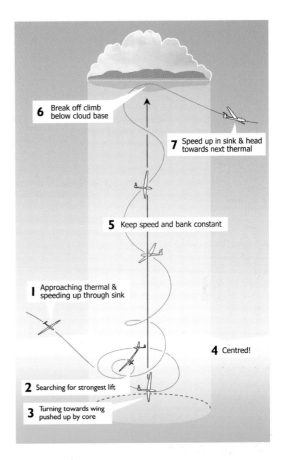

In a thermal.

example, if the general wind and the streeting were in the directions indicated by (1) in the illustration, then wave activity is unlikely. However, if streets form when the general wind is more or less at right angles to them (2), there is a high probability that wave is involved. When wave and thermal interact the results can vary a great deal, ranging from strong enhancement of the thermals in marked bands, to their complete suppression. The downgoing side of a wave can also stop a ridge from working.

THERMALLING RULES
• Gliders already established in a thermal have right of way
• Gliders entering a thermal shall circle in the same direction as gliders already established, or in the same direction as the glider with the nearest vertical separation

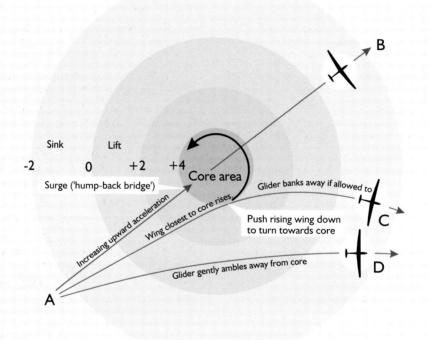

Thermal structure from above.

(this takes care of the odd occasion when a pilot from another universe insists on going the other way)

- The entry into a thermal should be planned so that the joining glider establishes itself on the opposite side of the circle to any other glider (nearest vertical separation again, but this may produce problems if more than one glider is at the same entry height. If so, better to move away and then come in again lower down)
- Keep a good lookout and always ensure adequate separation from other gliders (keep out of their blind spots if possible)
- Leave a thermal with the same care you entered it.

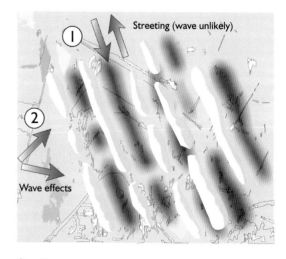

Streeting.

WAVE

In the 1930s glider pilots became aware that long after thermals had disappeared at the end of the day, very smooth lift could occur which carried them far beyond the heights to be expected from ridge lift alone. This lift was often accompanied by the appearance of lenticular-shaped clouds, which remained stationary even in strong winds, and so were unlikely to have much to do with thermals, which usually drift with the wind. This new and unusual form of lift could also be present when the sky was cloudless. There were many theories about what was going on.

Lee waves (usually referred to simply as wave) form downwind of hills when the atmospheric conditions are right, as described in the opening account of a wave flight. The lift is extraordinarily smooth and consistent, but something known as rotor can form in the area below the wave peaks, usually fairly low down, and give you a really wild ride. Wave is not solely dependent for its formation on solid hills. On many days, at a given altitude there will be a temperature inversion (effectively a lid on convection) and at that level an abrupt change either in wind direction or strength. Thermals may rise to the inversion altitude, protrude through it, and have the same effect on the upper

wind as solid hills, triggering off what is known as shear wave. Shear wave is great fun to find and use (getting into it can be tricky), and it isn't always very strong, nor does it often extend very high above cloudbase. As a cross country resource its use is limited.

Gliders use wave by tracking along the upgoing part of the wave much as they would track along the flank of a hill. Apart from the obvious differences, wave can involve wind speeds of more than 40kt at altitude; the sort of speeds which no-one would dream of taking off in, let alone getting the glider out of the hangar. These wind speeds are only a problem if there is little or no cloud associated with the wave, when there are few reference points to help you maintain station. It is relatively easy to drift backwards over the wave's crest into the sinking air on the lee side. If there are clouds, as is usually the case, their shape will give a good clue as to where the strongest wave is, and the wave's orientation – parallel to and downwind of the hills creating it – can be spotted once you're above cloudbase, but it isn't always obvious until then. Not only are tremendous heights possible (see records later), but so are long distances at very high speeds.

Wave in New Zealand. The wind is blowing from left to right. A. WATSON

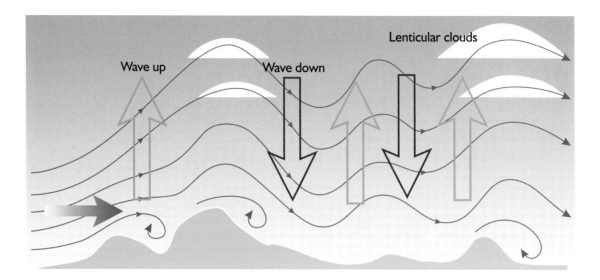

Lee waves.

CLOUD FLYING

Most of the world's current height records have been gained in lee waves, but there was a time when cloud flying was the accepted way to reach high altitudes. Unfortunately, the really big clouds required are very likely to be thunderstorms. Climb rates exceeding 2,000ft/min – a vertical velocity of 23mph – are common, but 6,000ft/min has been clocked, which is very nearly 70mph. Regrettably, being struck by lightning is not always an illuminating experience and the likelihood of structural damage in the more turbulent areas of such clouds is high.

The overwhelming majority of clouds are neither monstrously dyspeptic nor electric, and cloud flying is an interesting skill to acquire. The need to go higher in order to go farther has almost disappeared because of improved glider performance, so the skill is not much cultivated these days.

The UK is one of the very few countries in the world that still allow gliders to cloud-fly. Should you decide to try it get some decent practical tuition first. It is possible to teach yourself, but the method is hit and miss. Most gliders have no more than the basic instrumentation necessary, which is the ASI, a T/S and a variometer. A compass is useful even though it will spend most of its time spinning round and round. There is a consistent pattern to such wayward behaviour, so in principle the instrument is usable.

WEATHER FORECASTS

The types of lift we've looked at are all down to the weather, but this book won't attempt to describe how that works. If you are serious about gliding you will learn all about it first hand, and discover, if you didn't know it already, that forecasts are not very reliable!

Most forecasts are aimed at people who want to know whether it will rain or not, and how cold it's likely to be. Gliding forecasts need to be much more specific. When will useable convection (lift) begin? When will it stop? Tell me cloudbase. Will the visibility be good? Are there going to be sea breezes? Is it worth going to the airfield at all? Why don't you know the answers? ... and so on and so forth. If you've just begun learning to glide you won't need super soaring conditions, nice as they are. The less than perfect gliding weather which is normal in the UK is, in terms of basic training, much more useful because it offers opportunities to brush up on circuits and landings and, as always, co-ordination. It is utterly pointless clocking up hundreds of hours of soaring if you have so little practice at taking-off and landing that you can't do either very well.

It pays to be able to interpret weather charts for yourself. Given the inaccuracy of most forecasts this might sound like an impossible task – if the professionals are having problems getting it right, what chance have you got? Even the best glider pilots can completely misread the weather,

The Dee valley, looking west from Aboyne.

but less frequently than everyone else, so it is possible to be right more often than chance. You just have to work at it. Think of it this way; the forecaster does all the hard work collecting the information and it is up to you, given your knowledge, to assess the chances of the forecast being correct. One way to help you is to compare forecasts with what actually happened! The devil will appear not in the type of weather so much as the timing of its arrival.

What is a 'good' gliding day?
The ideal days are those where lift is in abundance and easy to find, cloud bases are high, the day is long, visibility is good, it isn't too hot, the wind is light – and you are on the airfield, able to fly, top of the flying list and have a glider available. Such a perfect day arrives once in a blue moon, but there are many other days when excellent flights are possible.

What exactly are you looking out for? Briefly, the air mass needs to be unstable, which means that it will encourage convection, but not to the extent that the show gets wildly out of hand and produces large amounts of cloud, heavy showers or thunderstorms. The impressive

cloud illustrated on page 133 is on the hefty side and about ten minutes after the photograph was taken a small funnel cloud appeared out of the base and then disappeared again. Later it rained hard. Nor do you want a very dry air mass, which produces no cloud and is the cause of some of the so-called 'blue' days. These are not always as difficult as described in the introduction, but it is easier if cumulus type clouds mark where the thermals are. At a gliding site where wave is frequent, the criteria for the good day might be somewhat different.

The characteristics of an air mass depend on where it has come from. Air from the Azores (Maritime Tropical) will be warm, contain a lot of water vapour, be fairly stable (ie doesn't encourage convection) and hazy. Air from the Arctic Circle (Direct Maritime Polar) will be cold, relatively dry, and moderately unstable. Returning Maritime Polar, on the other hand, won't be that good because having spent a long time over the ocean it will have been warmed up and carry quite a lot of water vapour (see diagram on page 133).

The various air masses meet and weather fronts mark the mixing zones between them. A warm front occurs when a warm(er) and less dense air mass follows a cold(er) and

131

Distant cumulonimbus cloud.

denser one, riding up over it along a slope several hundred miles long and giving rise to characteristic cloud formations; high streaks of cirrus first, then a gradually lowering and thickening of the cloud until eventually rain falls. The weather ahead of a warm front deteriorates fairly slowly. A warm front can take a long time to clear the country, and the visibility and soaring conditions in the trailing warm sector are often poor. Warm fronts are represented on weather charts by a thick line with lots of semicircles.

Cold air masses which are following warmer ones tend to catch them up and then, being more dense, drive underneath the warmer air mass and lift it up, often creating highly unstable conditions, such as thunderstorms. The weather can deteriorate very rapidly ahead of a cold front and clear equally quickly behind it. Good weather can follow, but this depends on how active the front was, and on the barometric pressure behind it, which for preference should be rising. The cold front is represented on a chart by a thick line with lots of small triangles.

The first weather chart (below) represents an indifferent day for cross country flying. Though the wind was light, the air mass had moved slowly towards the UK from the direction of High V, over some of the most industrialized areas of Europe. As a result, the air was full of industrial

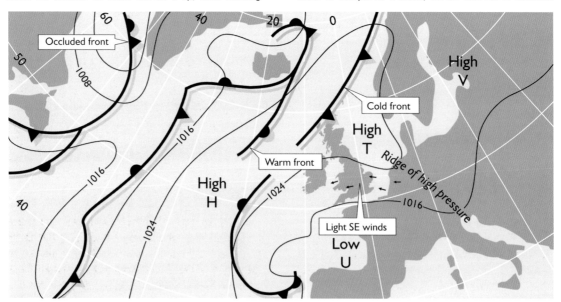

Synoptic chart for an indifferent day.

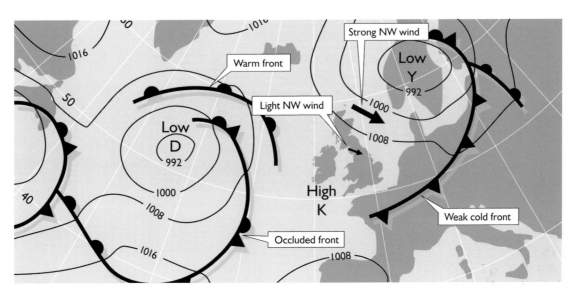

Synoptic chart for an excellent day.

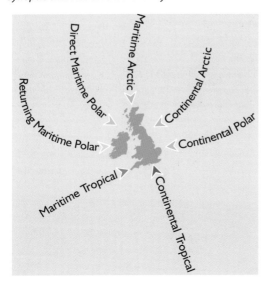

Air mass direction.

Impressive cloud.

murk – another factor that has be taken into account – and visibility was poor. By contrast, the second chart (above) represents an excellent day with high cloud bases, reliable thermals and a light wind. The chief things to note are that the weak cold front over the continent had crossed the UK from NW to SE during the previous afternoon, and behind it the pressure rose slightly.

These very brief descriptions can give you no more than the merest taste of what is involved in predicting the weather – a task which is far more difficult to master than learning to fly well. The key point as far as the weather is concerned is to watch the forecast carefully the day before you want to glide, and also to anticipate and be ready for the good days as far as you possibly can.

11 Glider Performance

When a glider pilot talks about a glider's performance he or she will be talking about four related things, and more or less in this order:

1) How far will it glide from a given height (the best glide ratio)
2) The glide ratio at high speeds
3) The slowest vertical velocity at which it will sink through the air (minimum sink speed)
4) How it handles. Is the response to the controls sluggish, heavy, light, are the airbrakes effective or not... and so on

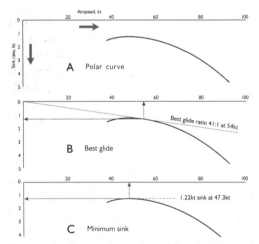

The polar (performance) curve, best glide and minimum sink.

THE PERFORMANCE CURVE

Apart from the handling, the glide ratio and the minimum sink form part of a general performance curve known (incorrectly) as a polar curve. At any given speed a particular glider will be gradually descending through the air at a particular rate. For example, it might be flying along at 60kt and sinking at, say, 2kt. The glide ratio is, among other ways of calculating it, the forward speed divided by the sink rate, which in this case is 60/2 or 30:1. If the glider is flown at various speeds and the associated rates of sink measured, the two can be plotted on a graph, giving rise to a characteristic curve.

Any tangent to the polar drawn from the zero, as illustrated opposite, will give you the best glide ratio for a particular glider, and the speed at which this occurs. Aircraft are afflicted by two major forms of drag, one of which increases with speed while the other decreases. There is an airspeed where the total drag of these two is at its lowest possible value. Flying faster or slower than this speed increases the total drag, and as a result the glide ratio at any other airspeed can only be worse. If the speed and sink axes are to the same scale (i.e. one millimetre represented one knot along both axes), then any line drawn from the zero to just clip the curve, as illustrated, will be a literal representation of the shallowest possible slope down which the glider can run. It will also tell you at what speed this occurs. If you divide the speed at the point where the

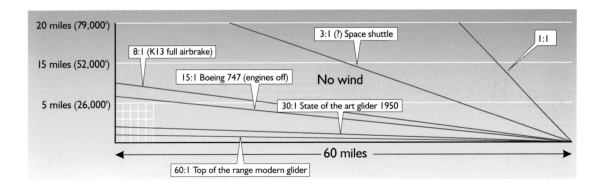

Glide ratios compared.

tangent touches the curve by the sink rate at the same point – in this case 54/1.32 – the glide ratio is 40.9:1. In still air this glider will at best travel 40.9 miles for every mile of height lost.

The diagram above compares the glide ratios of several aircraft, including the Space Shuttle, which must have the worst glide ratio of any glider ever built. The minimum sinking speed is slower than the best glide speed, and fairly close to the stalling speed. As with the best glide ratio you can find a value for the minimum sink from the polar. It is the highest point on the curve. From the example on the previous page its value is 1.25kt at 47.5kt (this gives a glide ratio at that speed of 38:1). In still air, flying at the speed for minimum sink will give you the longest airborne time from any height.

MINIMIZING DRAG, MAXIMIZING LIFT

Regardless of the increasing use of computers to model airflow, aerodynamics still remains something of a black art, particularly in glider design. That's not to suggest that designing a glider is largely guesswork, far from it, but gliders look simple. Their cockpits are uncluttered in comparison with those of powered aircraft; their lines clean and smooth, and their structures so devoid of obvious nuts, bolts and joins that they resemble nothing so much as a series of elegantly curved boxes. One might be tempted to think that it was therefore very easy to get good performance. However, the simplicity of a modern glider's looks belies its aerodynamic sophistication and it still relies for

that final edge of excellence on the intuition and experience of the designer.

Efficiency is a measure of the ratio between what you put in and what you get out. Bad features of powered aircraft can sometimes be hidden by thousands of horse-power, but gliders need to move through the air causing as little disturbance as possible, and so the aerodynamics have to be spot on. The shape of the glider, particularly the wing, and the material out of which it is made, are important to keep the drag levels as low as possible. That way the best glide ratio will be as large as possible and the gliding performance at high speeds may also be signifi-cantly better.

In common with early aircraft, gliders were first made out of wood and fabric. As well as needing to be strong and light, the structure must be as smooth as possible. Wood is a good material with which to work, but even if you begin with a smooth surface, after a few years of use it usually starts to ripple. Since the exact shape of any aerodynamic object is important to its efficiency, any unintentional bumps and lumps will reduce this, sometimes drastically. Many older wooden and even metal gliders develop a slightly rippled surface over time – referred to occasionally as the 'starved horse' look. It's not dangerous, but the glider won't perform as well as it did when new.

One of the biggest changes in glider design was the introduction of GRP (glass reinforced plastic). Fibreglass, as GRP is usually referred to, had been used for non–struc-tural items in many post war gliders, but the first to be built entirely from GRP was the 16m Akaflieg Phönix, which first flew in 1957. The glider was made in sandwich fashion,

The world's first GRP glider, the Phönix.

with each component comprising two layers of fibreglass enclosing a layer of balsawood. Though light and strong, balsawood is an organic material susceptible to mould and rot. The basic techniques of modern GRP construction have not changed much – each major component is built in two halves in moulds, and then stuck together like an Airfix kit, but some of the materials used are different. Carbon fibre is now very common and the 'sandwich' layer is made of polyurethane foam. GRP enables gliders to be light and strong and consist of curves, which would have been hard to create to the required level of accuracy in wood or metal. The modern glider is one of the most seamless and efficient flying machines you will ever come across, with an extraordinarily smooth surface finish and a genuinely 'stable structure' that will stay the shape the designer intended for a very long time. There have been other changes too which have helped glider performance improve, one of which is a much better understanding of how air moves over surfaces.

RETRACTABLE UNDERCARRIAGES AND FLAPS

The sole reason for having a retractable undercarriage is to reduce drag. In the early days of gliding many gliders took off and landed on a sprung skid. A few had a droppable undercarriage, which was released shortly after take-off, and the glider then landed on a skid. Almost without exception, these days modern high performance single seat gliders have retractable undercarriages.

Flaps work by changing the shape of the aerofoil of which they form a part (see diagram on next page), and have a number of purposes:

- To provide extra lift and lower the stalling speed. This allows slower approach and landing speeds and smaller circles in thermals
- To provide extra drag, usually as an aid to approach control
- To reduce, by using negative flap, one particular form of drag which increases with speed

EFFECTS OF WIND ON GLIDER PERFORMANCE

To cover the greatest distance in completely still air you just fly onwards at the airspeed which gives you the best glide ratio. As with landings, the wind has a large effect, not on your glide angle through the air, but in relation to the ground. For example, if you fly downwind you will cover a lot more ground than you will upwind. But, by the same token, the speed at which you fly upwind to make the maximum distance over the ground (or to reach a fixed point upon it, such as the gliding field) is not the same speed you need to fly for maximum distance downwind. Take a silly example. The wind is 40kt and your glider's best glide speed happens to be the same. If you fly downwind at 40kt you will travel over the ground at 80kts, and if you fly upwind at 40kt you will travel over the ground

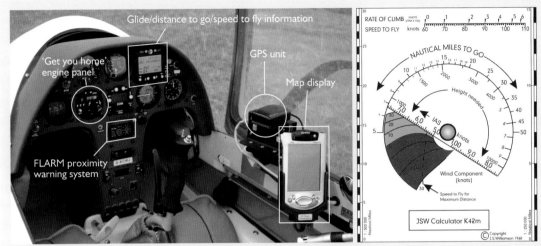

The JSW calculator is about half the size of the map display in the photograph

Electronics and a JSW (John Williamson) glide calculator.

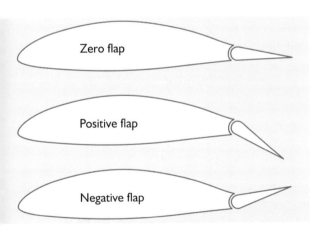

Flaps.

A modern two-seater, the Duo Discus.

at 0kt! If your glider's sink rate at best glide is 1.3kt and you begin from one mile high, then you will travel 80/1.3=61.5NM downwind (71 statute miles), and 0/1.3NM upwind, which is nowhere.

Obviously, if you fly faster into the wind then even though the glider's sink rate will increase, you will begin to move forward and your glide angle over the ground will improve, as it must from zero! At some point you will reach a speed where the glide angle over the ground is at a

maximum, and if you go any faster than that it will start to deteriorate again. You need the glider's polar to work all this out. Modern electronic equipment can do the calculations at the press of a button or three, but the far cheaper, portable, and entirely battery-free JSW calculator will do most of them, if you can find one. It does require a bit more user effort than finger jabbing. Make sure the K number (see figure) is either the same as or very close to the best glide ratio of your glider.

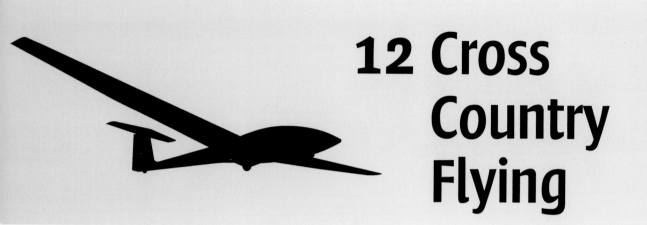

12 Cross Country Flying

THE BIG CHALLENGE AND ITS REWARDS

The challenge of cross country flying is to take a weather forecast, see the potential in the day's weather, and then design a flight to various distant waypoints that keep you in the good weather and will take you as long to complete as the soaring day lasts. Easy? If the weather is good for soaring, almost anything is possible if the day is long enough. Something which becomes very clear when you fly in the UK is that this country is small, so fitting really long flights into its confines requires ingenuity.

A typical turning point, Didcot Power Station.

Success in cross country flying requires soaring skills, ability to read the weather, good navigation and a degree of stamina. Cross country flights that fail tend to come unstuck for two reasons:

1) The weather either wasn't as good as forecast or where it was forecast to be – which amounts to the same thing
2) Tactical errors, the most common of which are pushing on when perhaps you ought to be holding back, or consistently going to the wrong place in the sky

'Task' is a dreadful word for cross country flying, and can suggest to non-glider pilots that what is an interesting, if not always ecstatic experience, is compulsory fun (i.e. not fun at all). The 'task' word apart, the basic and most common type of cross country these days is a closed circuit. You take off from your base, fly round up to three declared turning points, and then land back where you started.

The illustration on the next page is a kind of table-top cross country. The pilot has declared a triangular task (say 300km) and launches by aerotow (1) at 11:30, setting off immediately after release at 3,000ft towards the nearest cumulus cloud on track to the first turning point. The first climb is slow and doesn't go very high. A better looking cloud beckons ahead and, though low, the pilot sets off towards it, contacts the lift and climbs quickly to what is still a fairly low cloud base. The next cloud provides weak

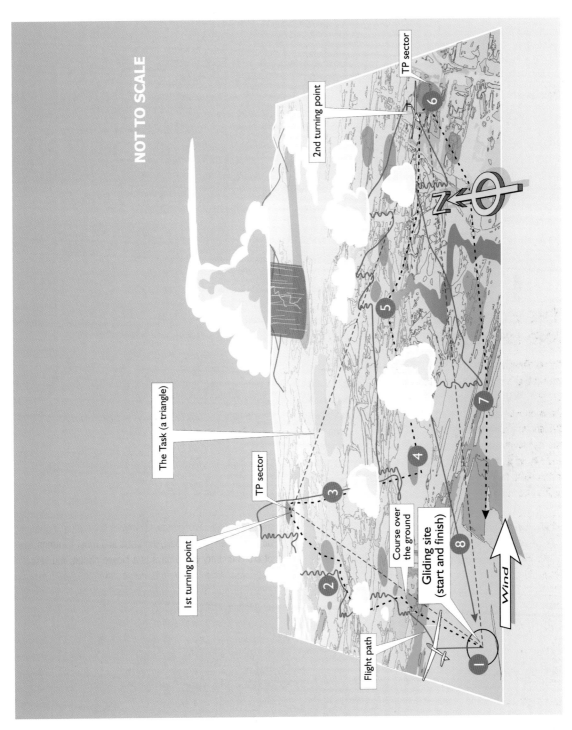

NOT TO SCALE

2nd turning point

TP sector

The Task (a triangle)

1st turning point

TP sector

Flight path

Course over the ground

Gliding site (start and finish)

Wind

A cross country flight.

lift again. Pressing on after a short climb the pilot then encounters strong lift and climbs quickly, moves on again and just before the first turning point (TP) contacts a thermal that carries the glider to cloud base, now higher than before. The glider rounds the TP, either photographing it from the designated sector or, far more commonly these days, relying on GPS to indicate transit through it, with an onboard data logger recording the glider's height and track as 'evidence'. One challenge of long flights is that an early start can mean setting off with weak lift and low cloud-bases. Days can stay that way and cloud spacing be so critical that even if only one fails to 'work', you won't reach the next before you're on the ground. Good gliding conditions can be confined also to quite small areas, and, airspace apart, where they are may not always be where you want to go. There is that sort of problem today, and the glider now sets off towards a distant cloud well to the right of the intended track.

The area between (3) and (5) looks more or less dead, partly as a result of the lake areas, but largely because of the thunderstorm sitting over the hills. The glide from (3) to (4) proves long and again the glider gets low. The climb at (4), though, is good. By the time the glider reaches the second TP at (6) the cloud base is much higher than previously and a quick calculation suggests that a straight glide back to the airfield is now possible. However, on the way the glider flies into strongly sinking air and is only saved from landing out at (7) by a strong thermal which carries the glider up until it is once again within range of the airfield. Climbing slightly higher than required, the pilot sets off (8) towards the finish line, arrives back at 15:25 and lands shortly afterwards.

Time for the task – 3hr 55m. Distance 300km. Average speed 76.5 kph – very good indeed for a wooden glider, OK for a fibreglass glider, but would have been faster without the big misjudgement of height needed for final glide home from (6) – forgot about the headwind, perhaps? Possible tactical error between (3) and (5), should have gone straight from one to the other and not via (4).

First Cross Country

Your first cross country flight will probably be either in a two-seater or the Silver Distance badge flight when you are solo. By the standards of what you may do eventually, this is quite a short flight, but much of the preparation required for it will apply to all the others, however long or short they are. The first requirement for the Silver Distance is a suitable day. Cloud base needs to be above 3,000ft, at least, and cumulus should mark thermals which are both reliable and frequent. The wind should not be too strong. Visibility also needs to be good so that navigation is straightforward.

On the day there is, even before you fly, quite a lot of preparation. Some of this can be done weeks in advance, such as deciding your goal (have several options worked out). There are launch height limitations based on the distance you are going to fly, which need to be worked out beforehand if you are not to inadvertently deny yourself the badge. On the day, as part of the preparation to validate the flight you will need access to a barograph or a data logger (an electronic barograph), both of which record height against time. Most data loggers also record positions. You might need a camera as back-up or as final proof that you went where you said. Permission to go cross country will be needed from the duty instructor and a suitable briefing, not necessarily from the same person. Most clubs provide lectures during the winter which cover every aspect of badge flights and early cross country flights, and will give you all the grounding you need in what's required and how to go about getting it.

Flying Faster – Why Bother?

The perfect task would exactly fill the soarable day, but the length of that day will only be known with certainty when it is over. Any task that you set yourself has to allow for that, so it isn't always a good idea to plan to start on the day's first thermal and arrive back on the last, because you may have no idea where either of them are likely to be. The outlanding risk at the start is also very high – and potentially very embarrassing.

For longer tasks, such as the Gold Distance (300km) the length of the soaring day – which can be up to ten hours but is more likely to be about eight – can be a critical factor, and so will be your average speed. If during shorter cross countries you have averaged 50kph, then in eight hours you ought to be able, theoretically, to travel 400km. Likewise, if your average speed overall was about 70kph,

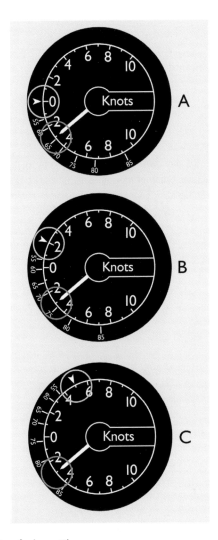

MacCready ring settings.

then 560km should be possible in eight hours, remembering, of course, that a day may start and end with weak lift, but be very strong during the middle hours. To begin with your average speeds will be slow to the point of standstill. When the writer began cross country flying, he managed to do one downwind task at an average speed slower than that of the prevailing wind, which takes some doing. For yourself, keep a record of cross country distances and times because, based on those results, you can more easily work out whether a flight you are planning on a given day is possible or not.

SPEED-TO-FLY THEORY

A crucial factor in successful cross country flying is to fly at the correct speeds. When you fly from one thermal to the next the air in between is anything but still. Indeed, it may be going down quite fast. It is important to avoid areas of sinking air if you can, but a lot of the time you won't know exactly where they are. Nevertheless, you need to pass through them quickly, and there's a problem. If you fly faster you come down more quickly, and since you are already in sinking air that adds to the glider's sink rate – so the overall sink rate can be high. On the other hand, if you slow down to prevent the glider sinking quite so fast, you then spend more time in the sinking air and lose just as much height! What to do? Somewhere between the two there must be a speed to fly that gets you through the sink as quickly as possible, but with minimum loss of height.

Around the outside of most variometers there is an adjustable ring marked with a set of speeds. These are based on the polar curve for the glider and are your speed-to-fly calculator. For example, say that the ring is set as in example (A). As you fly into sinking air the variometer registers 3kt down. The speed opposite that is 65kt. If you fly at that speed you will pass through the sink in the optimum time. If the sink increases the ring will tell you to speed up and vice versa. There's slightly more to it than that because the ring can be adjusted to allow for the effects of rising air, also crucial to your cross country speed.

'Speed-to-fly' theory is based on a very simple model, that of a glide followed by a climb. Theoretically your overall cross country speed is a measure of how long it takes you to get from point (1) to point (2), and then climb to point (3). So the faster you fly between (1) and (2), and the quicker you climb from (2) to (3), the higher your average speed. But you have here the same problem, in a slightly different guise, as you had with the sinking air – you don't know the strength of the thermal until you get there. If you knew that, then you could fly at a speed appropriate to the expected rate of climb – slowly towards a weak thermal (to conserve height) and fast towards a strong one which will give you a better climb rate to make up for the height lost due to speed. For example, if the lift was going to be 5kt, you would set the ring's zero next to +5kt on the variometer, and then just fly the indicated speeds. In this case, 3kt of sink (C) would equate to an airspeed speed of over 80kt. If you then arrive at the

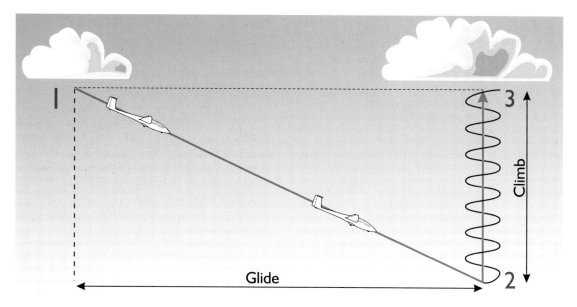

Basic speed to fly theory. Glide and climb.

thermal and find only 1kt, you've blown it because, unless you have sufficient height to reach the next thermal, you are now committed to a slow and laborious climb to make up at least some of the height you just threw away.

As you don't know the strength of the thermal upon which your average speed depends until you've already done the crucial glide to reach it, some allowance needs to be made for getting it wrong. Practical experience shows that if the thermals on any given day are averaging about 3.5kt (in reality that's your average rate of climb), you should fly towards each with a ring setting of a half to a third that value, ie about 1.5kt. The chances are that the thermal will be no less than that and quite possibly better. If you do the sums, you will discover that as long as the ring setting is greater than 0 (even 0.5 makes a big difference), but not hugely greater, you won't lose out too much on the overall speed and, just as importantly, won't fly yourself into the ground or have to commit yourself to a very slow climb just to remain airborne.

CONSERVING HEIGHT

A different situation, where staying airborne is more important than going fast, would be finding yourself in an area with no lift of any kind – and yes, it can happen. Let's say that you are at 3,000ft. A mile or two away the sun

breaks through the unbroken stratus cloud and lights up a small patch of ground. If the day was soarable previously and the air mass has not changed, it's a good bet that this spot of warming sunlight will eventually produce another thermal, but you won't know exactly when. It could pay to hang about over or slightly downwind of this pence-worth of sunshine and wait. If you fly around at the speed for minimum sink, and minimum sink is 1.1kt, then you will be losing 110ft/min and it will take 20 minutes for you to descend to 1,000ft. By then the thermal may have kicked off. Flying faster than minimum sink may take you further, but in this instance will simply cause you to land out sooner.

NAVIGATION

Reading and using a map

The important maps are the 500,000:1 (referred to as the '1/2-million') and the 250,000:1 ('1/4-million'). The 1/2-million contains all the airspace information you're ever likely to need, Notams apart (see later note), a legend explaining exactly what all the symbols and acronyms mean, but lacks the finer detail you might need if you were lost, or trying to skirt closely a restricted area. The 1/4-

million contains occasionally overpowering amounts of detail, but its chief drawback is that it doesn't show any of the airspace above 5,000ft. Most glider pilots use the 1/2-million map for the airspace, but for early forays across country it is not ideal (views vary on this), and to begin with you're probably best off carrying both.

Plotting a course is straightforward. Given a decent weather forecast you decide where you will go, and then draw on the map the track lines to whatever turning points or scenes of interest you've chosen. It is useful to use a felt tip pen to mark an arrow on the map indicating the prevailing wind direction. If the wind is light or if it changes markedly in strength and direction when you're airborne – something most likely to occur if you are fairly near to the

coast – it may not be much use. Working out and noting the magnetic headings of each track line is useful. However, calculating for drift is probably a waste of time as it's unlikely you will be able to fly any of the task legs in a straight line unless they happen to be straight up or down wind. A glider's fuel is height and needs regular topping up. Thermals are not fixed location filling stations in the sky, so a glider's path over the ground towards some distant point will almost always be a crooked line as the pilot seeks out the best areas of lift on the way, and tries to avoid the worst of the sink.

As for the flight itself, if you aren't using GPS (see later note) then you need to navigate by waypoints. In its simplest form this means that you set off in the right

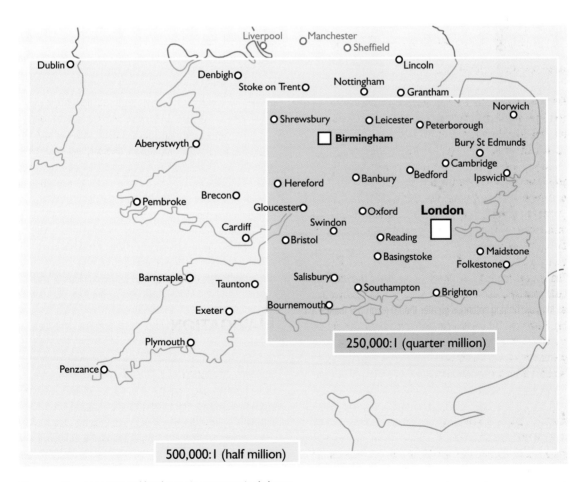

Comparative area covered by the main aeronautical charts.

Basic GPS unit.

Navigation using GPS – Global Positioning System

Using satellite positions and triangulating and comparing them with an internal database, a GPS unit can accurately and effortlessly fix your location and height to within about 6ft. A basic GPS is not that expensive and is relatively easy to use despite multi-function buttons. On entering the co-ordinates of your destination the GPS can tell you the course to steer to get there, the direction in which you are presently going, your current speed over the ground, the distance to go and how long it will be before you get there. The GPS can be linked to other instruments in the cockpit and provide readouts which tell you how high you need to be to reach the same point, your average speed, the latest news from Tibet and much else besides.

Wonderful though GPS is, the technology isn't quite as rock solid as one might wish. Everything works a treat if the batteries don't fail, the software doesn't play up, the GPS signals haven't been disrupted in some way, the weather is there to take you to your destination, and you have entered the correct coordinates. System malfunctions apart, it would not be a joke to say that GPS's chief drawback is the user.

Glider navigation requires a set of skills where the emphasis is on re-evaluating your position and track on a regular basis. GPS has certainly lightened the workload here as it will automatically work out where a turning point is in relation to you, and give you the course to fly to get to it.

Airspace and other restrictions

Virtually the entire UK is criss-crossed with airways and dotted with other areas of airspace where access to gliders is either restricted or forbidden (see diagram on next page). As you might expect, areas around major airports from ground level to many thousands of feet are forbidden to gliders. The upper and lower limits of the airways are marked on aeronautical charts as flight levels, which are described on pages 50–51. Other areas to steer clear of are Danger Zones (DZ) – these are usually military exercise areas so don't land in them unless you want to be run down by a tank or blown up – and Aerodrome Traffic Zones (ATZ), which encircle active airfields. ATZs can be entered if the pilot has radio contact with the airfield's air traffic control facilities and can obtain permission, or if there is some kind of emergency – imminent landing out is not counted as one.

direction towards some on-track feature which you have accurately located on the map. Once there you proceed to the next feature or set of features. In powered aircraft you would expect waypoints to turn up at specified times, but with gliders there are too many variables to make that a practical option. Instead, what you see is usually more important than when you see it.

In any event, you are required by law to take aeronautical charts with you if you are going to fly cross country, but they aren't needed if you are only flying locally.

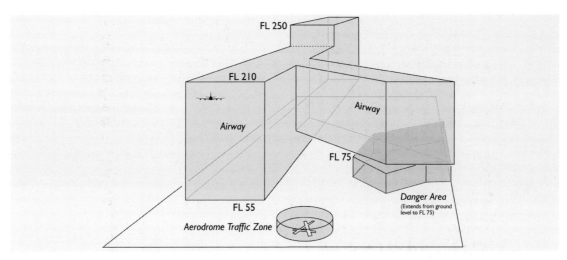

Airways and some other restricted airspace.

NOTAMs

Before flying cross country you must consult the 'Notifications to Airmen', or NOTAMs. They comprise a list of all planned aerial activity in the UK for the day (sometimes days) ahead, giving locations and times, and any unusual restrictions. Downloading and reading these obligatory notices in their badly presented native format can be a distressing experience. There are software programs available which help you make sense of the information, but it is worth pointing out that the CAA doesn't officially support any of them, though they may in the future. Notams include airshows, gliding competitions, parachuting, laser beam displays, military exercises and a lot more. Often at very short notice, they announce the establishment of purple airways for the protection of royal personages flitting from place to place. You can be prosecuted for some infringements. Flying through a Red Arrows Display or wafting through an active parachuting zone would have repercussions. Every club will display the Notams in a prominent place, and you must read them.

LANDING OUT

Part of your training covered how to do a good circuit and landing, and that entailed improving your judgement of height and position without reference to the altimeter. If applied correctly, the technique that you have been taught is completely independent of location – in other words it will work for a landing anywhere, regardless of what the altimeter may tell you.

Apart from that useful practical skill, outlanding also entails other preparations. Always carry enough money with you to pay for phone calls if you don't have a mobile phone. If your crew are late in arriving to pick you up it can get cold out in the fields, so take a sweater even if the day is sweltering. Carry a small number of skewers and thin nylon rope to help you tie the glider down. Don't leave the parachute on the wing as it may get damp if it rains or, far less likely, gets stolen.

FIELD LANDINGS

The four S's: size, slope, surface and stock

The first decision is the one to land. Don't leave this until the last moment unless you want to make things really difficult for yourself. During any cross country you should always be monitoring the areas over which you are flying, even if you are high. It is very unsound practice to keep blasting on as the trees come up to meet you, in the hope that at the last minute a suitable field will present itself. The 'suitable' field must be big enough to land and stop in, reasonably smooth, contain no deep crop or animals, have no slope (or as little as possible), and be free of obstructions both in the field and

Outlanding in the southern French alps. Very few landable fields available in these areas. J. BRIDGE

on the approach. During the period late May to early August, in areas where arable farming is the major activity (grain or oil-seed rape), suitable fields in which to land can be very few and far between.

Choose a field well in advance of having to land. On early cross countries you should start looking for likely fields when you are down to about 2,000ft above ground. At about 1,500ft look for lift only in the immediate neighbourhood of your chosen field. At about 1,000ft check the wind direction, look at the surface again, check for likely obstructions, and at 800ft begin the circuit, but try not to cramp it. You will attempt to make the largest field you can see (however small it really is) look as big as your home site, and since most fields are smaller than that you will keep edging in until it 'looks right'. This can lead you to start the approach far too high/close. Carefully monitor the RP and check the approach speed every few seconds. This can be difficult if you're about to land in a small field, but do it because it is far too easy to get too slow in your desire not to overshoot. Monitoring the ASI will also show if you are going too fast. Once the glider has touched down, stop as quickly as possible without tipping it on its nose. Never taxi up to a gate or anything else. You have no real idea what the surface is like and there may be a big hole you can't see, and even if you spot it you may not be able to avoid it.

ARE YOU A TRESPASSER?

You're an uninvited guest, so don't make yourself an unwelcome one as well. The overwhelming majority of farmers are helpful and understanding, but whatever recent laws may say regarding access, the farmer farms and looks after the land you're on, and it is his livelihood. As a matter of common courtesy, make every effort to contact him and don't just vanish whence you came, even though this is sometimes unavoidable. When you do contact the farmer or the landowner, explain the situation: you've landed out (minor and unintended emergency), and your crew will be arriving to pick you up at about such and such a time. Offer to pay for any phone calls you may make if you aren't carrying a mobile.

When you leave the glider to find the farmer, particularly if you have landed near a built up area, remove things like cameras or portable GPSs from the glider and take them with you. Close the clear vision panel and if you have brought the canopy cover, use it. Try not to damage crops or anything else on the farm when your crew arrive to pick you up.

RIGGING AND DE-RIGGING A GLIDER

Because gliders are (a) likely to land out and (b) there isn't always hangar space in which to put them (a big club can have over 100 gliders on site), they are made to be easy to put together and take apart (rig and de-rig). Most gliders comprise four main bits: the fuselage, the two wings and the tailplane. The wings slot through the fuselage and are located there by fuselage mounted lugs. One or more large pins (main pins) are inserted through the overlapping main spars to lock them together and in place. The tailplane, often mounted on top of the fin, slots onto lugs mounted on the sternpost – the vertical former running down the back of the fin – and is locked in place using a screw-in rod through the leading edge of the fin or a spring loaded peg.

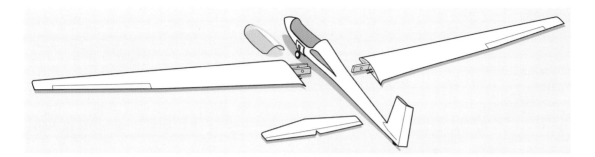

Disassembled glider.

The exact details of how everything fits and clicks together vary between types of glider. Most of the modern ones have controls which connect automatically when the glider is rigged; and automatically disconnect when it is de-rigged. This is not universal, so after rigging check that the controls are connected, and before de-rigging check if they need manually disconnecting first.

Some glider/trailer set-ups allow the pilot to rig and de-rig the glider without help, but usually rigging needs at least two people, and in the case of some of the much older gliders you might need six or more. Helping someone to rig is likely to be your first acquaintance with glider portability and, as you will discover, the wings are by far and away the heaviest item.

Checking the trailer and how the glider fits in it

As you become more involved in club activities you are quite likely to be asked to help in the retrieve of a glider which might have landed out a hundred miles away. Towing a glider trailer and the driving skills needed are not something for this book, but there are a few things you will need to know before you set off. Trailers can spend a lot of time on the airfield being neglected, so before every retrieve, check that the tyres are inflated to the correct pressure, that the lights, indicators and brakes work. Check that the number plate on the trailer is the same as the towing vehicle – it's a legal requirement.

Putting a glider into or taking it out of a trailer can be a cause of considerable damage if done incorrectly, so try and find out how everything works, at leisure, during the middle of the day, on the airfield, and not in the pouring

How the glider fits into the trailer.

rain and pitch darkness in a field in the middle of the night and nowhere. How do the fittings work? What goes in first? Are there wing trestles? What's the minimum number of people needed for the de-rig?

Look inside the trailer before leaving the airfield! In one famous example the crew arrived at the outlanding site, opened the trailer and found a glider already inside. Look inside also to make sure that the trailer contains all the necessary fittings. If you leave behind the cradle that is usually needed to support the fuselage, you will have problems.

Before leaving the site of any outlanding, make sure you've packed up everything both you and the pilot brought. Don't leave one of the main pins behind or something equally vital. If they are small items the farmer may have inadvertently ploughed them in before you get back.

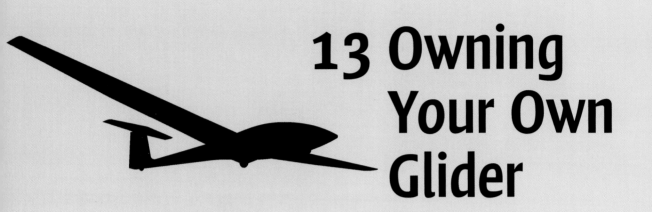

13 Owning Your Own Glider

WHAT'S YOUR AIM?

Do you want to compete, show off, enjoy flitting around the site or just fly off into some distant part of the country and probably get lost? State-of-the-art gliders aren't cheap. They are precision pieces of equipment built to very high standards and not in any great numbers. Despite modern techniques and materials, building them is labour intensive and the simple economics of their manufacture means that there is no way that they could be cheap. However, there is a flourishing secondhand market in older gliders, and even though you may not get the quick and slick performance of the latest supership, the older glider may fit your needs very well indeed, and at a fraction of the cost.

SPOILT FOR CHOICE

Glider prices can vary enormously, but you pay a hefty premium for performance. A modern high performance 15m glider, fully equipped with trailer and instruments, can set you back many thousands of pounds. Very few people can afford the money involved on their own if they want to have three meals a day, so most gliders are owned by syndicates of anything between two and four people. Much more than four and you may not get to fly your investment very often, unless you've bought a two-seater and modern two-seaters are very expensive indeed. There are some

very good and relatively inexpensive wooden gliders available, and the earlier generation of fibreglass gliders are also relatively cheap. There are very cheap gliders to be had, but on the whole their performance leaves something to be desired.

Costs of private ownership, advantages and disadvantages

Most people go into private ownership to be able to choose when they can fly. The drawback with club aircraft is that on the good days you're not the only one wanting to use them. Because most of us are civilized people there are flying lists, and because none of us would be able to take off without help from others with similar aims, we take it in turns to fly the club gliders. Naturally, when the good soaring days arrive there will be several people all wanting the same glider. Some clubs ballot for them in the morning or pilots book them weeks in advance, but for private owners, convenience and availability count above almost everything. They rarely if ever do the sums in any great depth because they've already decided on what they're going to do. Any argument to the contrary (a social one, for instance) is effectively irrelevant.

However, if after you've gone solo and had at least a year's experience (clubs vary in what you need before you're allowed to get your own glider) and are serious

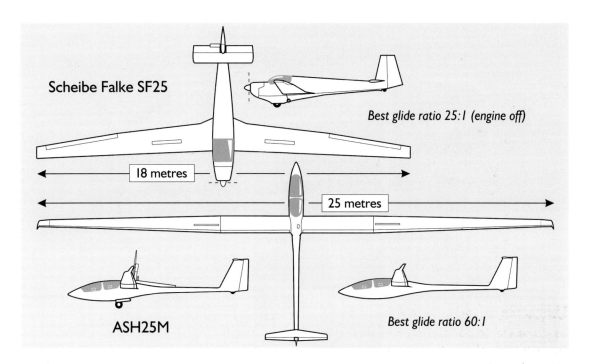

Scheibe Falke SF25

Best glide ratio 25:1 (engine off)

18 metres

25 metres

ASH25M

Best glide ratio 60:1

Glider with a 'get you home' engine and a motor glider.

about forming or joining a syndicate, start by doing the sums. There is no such thing as flying for free, even if all you do is leap out of your bedroom window flapping a bed sheet. The capital cost of the glider is the largest part of the equation. You MUST have insurance, even if it is only third party, but the full cover premium is based on the glider's hull value and, to some extent, that is based upon how desirable a glider it is – the secondhand value will give you a clue. For example, a wooden glider, though cheap to buy, may have a premium not that far short of that of a modern GRP glider, partly because repairing or rejuvenating wooden aeroplanes is, like thatching, a bit of a dying art. In addition you are paying the usual club fees. As against that you are not paying the club any flying charges, only the launch costs. One effect of this can be the loss of flying income to the club. Most clubs get round this by charging for trailer parking, described by private owners as an iniquitous tax upon their independence and by the clubs as a justifiable fee for the amount of rateable ground the trailer is occupying. The debate is ongoing.

Joining and forming a syndicate

This is a bit like getting married, but without the fog of romance, and requires thought! Don't leap into the first syndicate available or form a new one unless you are very sure of, and like, the people with whom you will be conjoining yourself. Syndicate disputes, though rare, have the potential for being just as acrimonious as club politics, and just as capable of destroying your love of gliding. A good syndicate will make flying more fun, provide you with a ready made crew, a rewarding social life and help you avoid financial ruin. For reasons of space or launch availability most clubs restrict the numbers of privately owned gliders. You will almost certainly have to ask permission to bring another glider onto a club site – perhaps by writing to the club committee and certainly by talking to the CFI.

LOOKING AFTER A GLIDER

Gliders need looking after well and should be treated as pieces of precision equipment. All gliders are required to have an annual inspection (a combination of service and

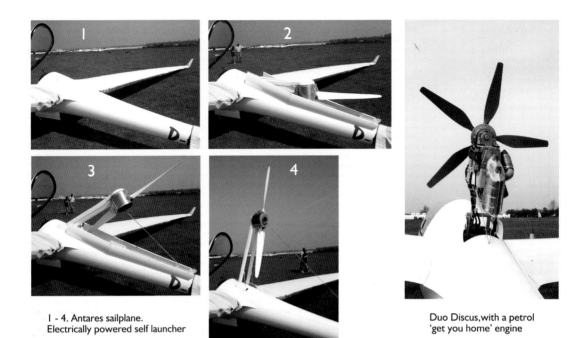

1 - 4. Antares sailplane.
Electrically powered self launcher

Duo Discus, with a petrol
'get you home' engine

A self-launching sailplane, and a sailplane with a 'get you home' engine.

Glider towout set-up.

A Falke motor-glider, used for navigation and field landing training, as well as air experience flights for young persons.

MOT) to ensure that they are (a) in good working condition and (b) to make them legal – in that order. As part of ongoing low-level maintenance throughout the flying year, always remove dust on the flying surfaces as it will reduce the performance. Clean the canopy regularly. What's the point of all that perspex and only a potentially panoramic view? Perspex is very easy to scratch, so don't wipe off any dust with a dry cloth. Lubricate very occasionally anything that needs lubricating. Do the daily inspections properly and don't become lax about them just because you 'flew the glider yesterday'. Maybe the mice made a meal of your parachute during the night, or nibbled their way through the electrics.

MOTOR-GLIDERS AND GLIDERS WITH MOTORS

Landing out isn't always one of the joys of gliding, but if you go cross country you will at some time land out. The weather may entice you miles from base with the promise of billowing cumulus and wonderful conditions ahead, then switch off as if a fuse had blown somewhere. You may just misread the day, over-value your expertise, and find yourself out of range of the home airfield and with no lift anywhere within reach. The obvious answer to not landing

out, apart from increased skills or not taking-off in the first place, is to equip the glider with a small retractable get-you-home engine, and gliders are increasingly so fitted – it's the power thing again!

Get-you-home engines give the luxury of self-retrieve, but with a caveat. Far less energy is required to keep a glider airborne than to get it off the ground, so if you do land out in a field and subsequently get the engine going you won't be able to take-off. You will either have to be aerotowed out or take a retrieve by road. There are pure gliders with self-launching capabilities, but to operate them you need a Private Pilot's Licence (not cheap), and for that and other reasons there aren't many self-launchers around. Motor-gliders are really light aeroplanes that happen to glide tolerably well when the engine isn't working. A popular aircraft with flying schools, the Cessna 150, has an engine-off glide ratio of about 7:1, whereas a motor-glider like the Falke (not especially effective either as a glider or a powered aircraft) manages anywhere between 22:1 and 30:1, depending on the version. Motor-gliders are particularly useful for cross country navigation and field selection training, and are increasingly used for some of the early training to solo, so you are quite likely to fly one at some stage in your gliding career.

14 Competitive Flying

COMPETITIONS

In order to improve your skills you need some yardstick against which to measure them, and one way (in fact just about the only way) to do that, is to compete. There are two (competing) points of view on the merits of competition. Some people think competition is terribly cruel and nobody should be allowed to suffer the trauma of second place (or much worse, third), while others are more loutishly Darwinian and think the more of it the better. Somewhere between those equally silly extremes there is useful and benign competition. By and large you won't

improve unless you do compete, even if it is only with yourself. 'I could have done that tight turn far better' is a form of competition, which leads to you practising how to improve your tight turns.

There are competitions at every level, from those between local clubs to world championships, but what do they actually measure? If you have two equally good pilots and one is flying a better performance glider than the other, the glider with the better performance can be flown faster round a given task and is more likely to complete it. Glider performance varies a lot. There are

Starting to launch the grid at a Regionals competition. J. BRIDGE

gliders in which you wouldn't dream of competing in the more high powered competitions because, no matter how skilled you were, you'd be back long after everybody else had gone home or you simply wouldn't complete the set task in the day available!

Given that not everyone has the same type of glider, the differences in their performance must be filtered out so that every pilot has an equal chance of winning. The measure is supposed to be the skill of the pilot, not that of the designer. The result is a scoring system that includes some handicapping, and has over the years grown more and more complicated in order to give every competitor a fair chance. In truth, if glider performances are too dissimilar there is no way that any workable handicapping system can ensure that everyone either starts or finishes on an equal footing. So, if you intend to compete on a national level you will need a glider whose performance is very similar to those of your competitors.

The broad division in competition gliding is between racing tasks, which at present form the overwhelming majority, and those where maximum distance is the key, either within a pre-specified time, or just simply as far as you can travel in the available soaring day. The last two types of task are not very popular with racing pilots because they are believed to depend rather more on luck than a task where everyone has to go round the same turning points in the same order, and more or less in the same weather. On the other hand it could be argued that the less restrictive tasks allow for the assessment of a wider range of pilot skills than the pure racing tasks, but if you're interested in competitions, go for those which suit your skills and temperament best.

THE NATIONAL LADDER

Of the other forms of competition available there is a National Ladder. Any time you do a cross country flight which is not part of a Regional or National competition, you can fill in a form at the club afterwards saying where you went and how quickly, and whether you declared the flight before you took off. Pre-declaration requires you to write down on the day who you are, the date, the time and where it is you intend to go. Give the declaration to another club member before you take off. Retrospective declarations are not allowed, and completed declared flights score more

highly than flights that are only partially completed or not declared beforehand. So, part of a pre-declared flight which you failed to complete because sea air had flooded in, say, and your second turning point was out of reach in the middle of all that, would not be a complete waste as far as scoring ladder points is concerned. However, the difference would be big enough to be disappointing! The pilot's word is taken for completing the task as declared, but if you want to win the ladder and gain a year's possession of the trophy, your qualifying flights need supporting evidence provided by photographs, or validated traces from an electronic logger or a standard barograph. Most glider pilots don't bother with such hassle, don't cheat and use the ladder solely to see how well they're doing in comparison to everyone else.

In order to take part in the high-level competitions, such as the UK National Championships, you have to start with the less high-powered competitions and earn yourself a place on the ratings list. There are very few places right at the top, in the British Team, for instance, but if you do consistently well over the years in the regional competitions then the rating system gradually squeezes you up the list towards the top places. This country has several World Champions who went through this rather long process to get there, but there is no other way to arrive on the pinnacle. If you are good enough and dedicated enough you may make it!

INTER-CLUB LEAGUE COMPETITIONS

Not everyone likes competitive gliding, although it is still possible to be very competitive about how non-competitive you are. The exact level of competitive intensity does vary, and some of the lower profile competitions can be both very instructive and hugely enjoyable. Gliding clubs are grouped together in regions and during the soaring season (April to September) each club in the region takes it in turn to host a weekend-long competition for that region. Each club fields three gliders and their pilots and crew. There will be a Novice (someone who has only just started cross country flying), an Intermediate (fairly experienced but with less than a specified number of hours and without certain badges), and the Pundit (anybody who is more experienced and falls outside the previous two categories). The scoring is based on speed and distance round set tasks, like Regional or National competitions, but points are awarded to each club for the weekend positions of their entrants. At the end of the year one club in the region will have more of these points than another and goes on to the Inter-Club League Final, there to wrestle for supremacy with the winners from the other regions. Competition is keen, but friendly.

ENTERPRISE-TYPE COMPETITIONS

Speed tasks are all very well, but cynics say that they are designed to make as little use of the soaring day as possible. Many pilots feel that this is not what gliding is all about, and that a rather less angst-ridden form of competition would be more interesting and instructive, and make far better use of the weather. Enterprise is a competition justly famous for its idiosyncratic scoring and creative task setting. The story goes that one task's turning point was a railway station. Nothing unusual about that, except that the photograph (which you were obliged to take in those days) had to show a train standing at the platform. This may suggest that Enterprise is frivolous, but that's not the case. It stretches and develops skills which many other competitions hardly seem to know exist. This rather free-wheeling style means that doing well in Enterprise does not count towards a placing on the ratings list. Nevertheless, you will fly more often than you might in a rated competition and probably learn a lot.

AEROBATICS

Gliders are designed to soar well and go cross country, and most are cleared only for simple aerobatic manoeuvres like the loop and the chandelle. Though many modern 15m gliders are strong enough to do some of the more advanced manoeuvres, they are relatively easy to over-speed and may be subject to other limitations. The margin between doing an advanced manoeuvre safely and having to bail out is too small for comfort. Nevertheless, a great deal of pleasure can be had out of the skilful execution of the simpler aerobatic manoeuvres. Always have some tuition first from an experienced instructor and don't try and teach yourself.

A few gliders are cleared for the full range of aerobatic manoeuvres and some clubs have aerobatics coaches. A national aerobatics championship is held every year at a different venue in the UK. It has even been known for gliders at airshows to perform aerobatics elegantly to music.

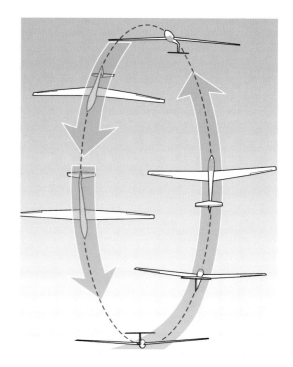

A loop.

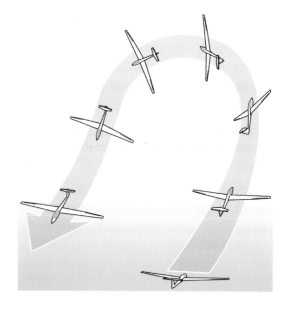

A chandelle.

Waiting for the grid to be launched.

WORLD AND UK GLIDING RECORDS

There are several classes of records, and separate ones for men and women. As would seem inevitable in such a competitive arena, the rules detailing what is or isn't a legitimate aim and claim, are labyrinthine. If you'd like to compete at the highest level, these rules will be a matter of interest. If you don't, they won't. There are National records, either Open (any span greater than 15m) or 15m classes, flown by UK born pilots anywhere in the world. There are also UK records (flown in this country) for the same classes. As a rough guide to what can be achieved in aeroplanes that have gravity engines and utilise the weather, there follows a small selection of some of the fastest, highest and farthest flights on the current (Jan 2012) FAI (Federation Aeronautique Internationale) and BGA databases. If you have Internet access you can log onto www.fai.org/gliding/records, or go the BGA's website at www.gliding.co.uk.

Height

The current world absolute height record (i.e. from sea level) stands at 15,460m (50,724ft). It was set on 26 January 2007 by Steve Fossett and Einar Enevoldson, flying a DG505 two seat glider. The flight was made from El Calfate, Argentina, peaking 12,000ft higher than the operating altitudes of commercial airliners. It required special preparation. Not only is the temperature at 15,000m about –70ºC, but the altitude is close to the point where, if you don't have a pressure suit, it doesn't matter how much oxygen flows into a face mask, you can't absorb enough to stay conscious. Both pilots wore heated pressure suits.

The UK absolute height record is 11,570m (37,961ft), held by Chris Rollings and Bryony Hicks flying a DG500 from the Deeside Gliding Club, Aboyne, Scotland on 08 October 1995.

Distance

The world free distance record is currently held by Klaus Ohlmann for a truly stupendous flight in 2004 of 3,009km (1,870 statute miles) in a Nimbus 4D, starting and finishing at San Martin de los Andes in Argentine (see map). This epic flight lasted 15hrs 08mins, and oscillated back and forth along a relatively short strip of the Andes.

In the UK the National free three turning point distance record stands at 1,020.07km (634 miles) and is held by Russell Cheetham flying an ASW22BL. On the same day, 26 June 2004, there were two other UK record flights (see UK map). In terms of sheer distance, John Williams, who has many other impressive records to his credit, flew 1,108.7km in an Antares 20E on 08 April 2007 – all in Scottish wave. Kay Draper holds the female UK free three turning point distance record with a flight of 762.6km in an LS8-18 on 30 July 2007.

Speed

These records are usually round closed circuit tasks, and there are records for 100km to 600km (in 100km steps), plus 750km and 1,000km. The fastest speeds are done abroad, mainly in South Africa or Australia, where gliding conditions can be fantastic, with cloud-bases well over 10,000ft and thermal strengths often in excess of 10kt (1,000 ft/min). Increasingly though, it is in wave where the longest and fastest distances are being done, with the Andes in South America offering the greatest scope - the entire chain is about 7,000km long. The limiting factors here seem to be the VNE of the gliders and the amount of daylight available. One thing to notice about the speeds is that most are greater than the UK's motorway speed limit.

Klaus Ohlmann holds the record for the fastest Open Class 500km triangle with a speed of 194.79kph (121mph!). The UK 500km Open Class triangle record gliders is held by Phil Jeffreys in a Ventus 2cxt-18, at a speed of 116.57kph (72mph). Sarah Kelman holds the feminine UK 500km triangle record with a speed of 86.21kph, flying an ASW28 on 15 August 1997.

Pamela Kurstjens holds the current National feminine record for a 1,000km out and return, flown in Australia at a speed of 133.89kph (83mph).

Duration

Duration records are no longer accepted.

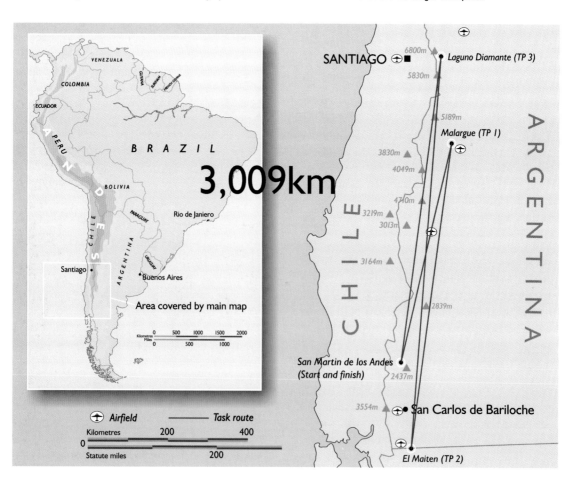

World distance record for gliders.

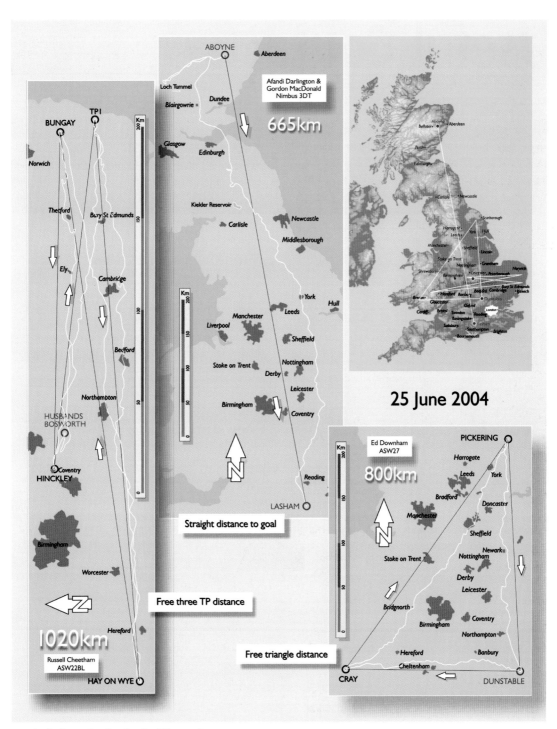

A particularly productive day for UK records.

Useful Contacts

Contacting the Clubs and the BGA

There are about one hundred BGA affiliated gliding clubs in the UK. A few of these are service clubs and have restricted membership, but if there is one near to you there's no harm in asking if they accept civilian members. The BGA can provide you with an up-to-date contact list of clubs, or you can visit the BGA's web site (URL below) where there is a clickable map showing where clubs are located, and which provides contact and other details. The BGA can be contacted by post or phone:

The British Gliding Association, 8 Merus Court, Meridian Business Park, Leicester, LE19 1RJ Tel: 0116 289 2956; www.gliding.co.uk

BGA Equivalents in Other Parts of the World

Virtually every European country has a gliding association, and the BGA can provide more information about each country's requirements in the way of medicals, licences and so on. European harmonization may have flattened out some of the parochial wrinkles, but member states still have their regulatory quirks. In France, for example, you are obliged to have your glider plastered with conspicuity markers, even though research conducted some years ago indicated that they aren't very effective. In a few countries the glider must be equipped with FLARM (an anti-collision warning system) if you intend flying in mountainous areas, and some countries (Netherlands) require gliders to be Mode S transponder equipped. The following is a selection of some international club addresses:

Australia
The Gliding Federation of Australia
130 Wirraway Road,
Essendon Airport,
Victoria 3041
Tel: (03) 9379 7411
www.gfa.org.au

Austria
Austrian Aero Club
www.aeroclub.at

Belgium
Belgian Gliding Federation
www.bgf.fcfvv.be

Canada
Soaring Association of Canada
Suite 107, 1025 Richmond Road
Ottawa
Ontario K2B 8G8
Tel: (613) 829-0536
www.sac.ca

Denmark
Dansk Svaeveflyver Union
www.dsvu.dk

Finland
Finnish Aeronautical Association
www.ilmailuliitto.fi

France
Federation Francaise de Vol a Voile
www.ffvv.org

Germany
Deutscher Aero Club e.V.
www.daec.de

Italy
Federazione Italiana di Volo e Vela
www.fivv.org

Netherlands
Royal Netherlands Aeronautical
Association Gliding Division
www.knvvl.nl

New Zealand
www.gliding.co.nz

Norway
Norsk Aero Klubb
www.nak.no

South Africa
The Soaring Society of South Africa
PO Box 1533
Rayton
1001
www.sssa.org.za

Spain
Royal Aero Club of Spain
www.rfae.org

Sweden
Swedish Soaring Federation KSAK
www.segelflyget.se

USA
Soaring Society of America, Inc
PO Box E
Hobbs
New Mexico 88241-7504
Tel: (001) 505 392-1177
www.ssa.org

Bibliography

BGA Instructor Manual 3rd Edition (BGA 2011)
BGA Modern Elementary Gliding (BGA 1978)
Gibbs-Smith *The Aeroplane, an Historical Survey*
   (HMSO, 1960)
Hardy, Michael *Gliders and Sailplanes of the World*
   (Ian Allan Ltd, 1982)
Irving and Welch *New Soaring Pilot* (John Murray, 1968)
Laurence Pritchard, J. *Sir George Cayley*
   (Max Parrish, London, 1961)

Longland, S. N. *Gliding – the BGA Manual 2nd Edition*
   (A&C Black, 2007)
O'Brien, T. and Turner, Charles *The Boys Book of Aeroplanes*
   (Grant Richards Ltd, 1912)
Piggot, Derek *Understanding Gliding* (A&C Black)
Welch, Anne *The Story of Gliding* (2nd edition)
   (John Murray, 1980)

Index

INDEX